How to Be a Good Savage and Other Poems

T0038802

How to
Be a Good
Savage
and Other
Poems

Mikeas Sánchez

Translated from Zoque and Spanish

by Wendy Call and Shook

MILKWEED EDITIONS

© 2023, "Note on the Translations," "Notes on the Poems," and English translation by Wendy Call and Shook
© 2006, 2012, 2013, 2019, Text by Mikeas Sánchez
© 2023, Introduction by Jake Skeets
© 2023, Cover art by Mary Austin Speaker
All rights reserved. Except for brief quotations in critical articles or reviews, no part of this book may be reproduced in any manner without prior written permission from the publisher: Milkweed Editions, 1011 Washington Avenue South, Suite 300, Minneapolis, Minnesota 55415.
(800) 520-6455
milkweed.org

Published 2023 by Milkweed Editions
Printed in the United States of America
Cover design by Mary Austin Speaker
Cover illustration by Mary Austin Speaker, based on a traditional Zoque glyph
Author/translator photos by Israel Gutiérrez, Axel Rivera, and Travis Elborough
23 24 25 26 27   5 4 3 2 1
First Edition

Library of Congress Cataloging-in-Publication Data

Names: Sánchez, Mikeas, 1980- author. | Call, Wendy, translator. | Shook, David (Poet), translator. | Sánchez, Mikeas, 1980- How to be a good savage and other poems. | Sánchez, Mikeas, 1980- How to be a good savage and other poems. Zoque. | Sánchez, Mikeas, 1980- How to be a good savage and other poems. Spanish.
Title: How to be a good savage and other poems / Mikeas Sánchez ; translated from the Zoque and Spanish by Wendy Call and Shook.
Other titles: How to be a good savage and other poems (Compilation)
Description: First edition. | Minneapolis, Minnesota : Milkweed Editions, [2023] | Series: Seedbank | "How to Be a Good Savage and Other Poems draws from Mikeas Sánchez's six published collections. All were originally published in bilingual Zoque-Spanish editions between 2006 and 2019, five in Mexico and one in Puerto Rico."--Note on the translations. | Summary: "In a fiercely personal yet authoritative voice, prolific contemporary poet Mikeas Sánchez explores the worldview of the Zoque people of southern Mexico"-- Provided by publisher.
Identifiers: LCCN 2023018006 (print) | LCCN 2023018007 (ebook) | ISBN 9781639550203 (paperback ; acid-free paper) | ISBN 9781639550210 (ebook)
Subjects: LCSH: Sánchez, Mikeas, 1980---Translations into English. | LCGFT: Poetry.
Classification: LCC PM4556.Z95 E5 2023 (print) | LCC PM4556.Z95 (ebook) | DDC 897/.43--dc23/eng/20230508
LC record available at https://lccn.loc.gov/2023018006
LC ebook record available at https://lccn.loc.gov/2023018007

Milkweed Editions is committed to ecological stewardship. We strive to align our book production practices with this principle, and to reduce the impact of our operations in the environment. We are a member of the Green Press Initiative, a nonprofit coalition of publishers, manufacturers, and authors working to protect the world's endangered forests and conserve natural resources. *How to Be a Good Savage and Other Poems* was printed on acid-free 100% postconsumer-waste paper by Sheridan Saline, Inc.

Matsa'koroya, Ramsés'koroya, dejurä kotzokyajpa'ankä teserike Shook'koroya, Wendy Call'koroya, jene sutkuy'jinh tzyiäj'kyajpa'ankä 'tyi'osykuy.

Para Matsa y Ramsés, por acompañarme en todo momento y con especial gratitud a Shook y Wendy Call, por su amor a la traducción.

For Matsa and Ramsés, for always being with me, and with special gratitude to Shook and Wendy Call, for their love of translation.

Contents

Introduction

As poets, we often trace words. Palabras. I traced the words throughout Mikeas Sánchez's stunning trilingual collection of poems, *How to Be a Good Savage and Other Poems*, finding possible translations of the word *word* into Zoque. The phrase *tzame* kept showing up again and again as I traced translations between *word* and *palabra* throughout the book. My journey was one of jump and leap, back and forth, through and beyond the words themselves. *Tzame* showed up in different iterations and appeared as a possible root or stem for larger concepts. For example:

    peka'tzame, possibly "ancient word"

    tzame'yomo'istam, possibly "some say"

    nhtzame, possibly "language"

Couched within these translations were other words: *power, knowledge, wisdom, world*. My interpretations might be inaccurate, but I am interested in the way in which the words glimmer at me through the text. Am I nearing a proper translation? But what even is proper when it comes to translating? Each poem and version refuses to hold its breath for the sake of correctness. As a whole, they are alive, distinct, and true, in stunning light across each page, faces turned from each other, keeping only echoes between them. And suddenly, the echoes gather as readers journey and search, traveling through space and time, generations and countries. Then, finally, comes a chorus: all the poems humming through the lark, harvests, red thunder, before returning to river, to sky. This book is about venture and dream, hope and home.

In Diné, *word* can be translated into *saad* (pronounced like *sawed*). However, the word itself is more stem and root than noun. For example, *saadtah* can mean "among words," while *saad baahózhǫ́* can mean "caring for the word." Most famously, *saad ei na'iiłná'* can mean "words move me and beyond me," which is a translation inspired by poets Rex Lee Jim and Manny Loley. However, translation takes some beam of light away from the Native word. *Saad*, I'm sure, is only conceptualized as *word*, but its direct translation is more rooted in the land itself. The syllable *aa* might exist in the way *tzame* exists. The *s* and *d* only shape the word *saad* into a version of what we might conceive of as *word*—after all, our brains might be thinking of only a written word, but Diné, like Zoque, only operates efficiently when spoken. The written form is a Western ideal, shaped by commerce and expansion. In that regard, *aa* could function the same as *tzame*, taking root and stemming in other larger concepts. For example:

hayoołkáál, or "very early morning"

ha'a'aah, or "skyward"

bizaad, or "language"

Like particles in the universe, syllables take shape, transform, filter, and code the reality around us. The words *breathing*, *light*, and *gravity*, for example, help us understand what conditions are necessary for existence. In her poems, Sánchez is both poet and physicist, singer and archeologist, mourner and analyst. Constellations of individual worlds are embedded by sound and syllable. It was the syllable, after all, that broke open poetry in the United States and allowed poets to depart from the romance of fixed form. Such a departure, however, is a returning for large numbers of poets and artists in the Americas who thrived before contact. American poetry has a long history of dynamism within verse and has been contributing to what we know as poetry for generations. Indigenous people have traced the word the way meteorologists trace weather patterns over the seas, forecasting the conditions and environments of the coming days. Poets are forecasters too. They tell of coming turmoil or blessing; they act as "archeologists of morning," as Charles Olson puts it. I think about a story told to me by Diné singer and thinker Herman Cody. He told me once that Tsinaajini, my first clan, comes from a group of people that often walked ahead of the main group, roaming the lands in search for possible danger. The word *Tsinaajini* translates into "Black Streak Wood People," for their place at the horizon. Tsinaajini as a people were often comprised of artists, weavers, singers, and storytellers, often only seen as silhouettes, black-streaked woods, forecasting conditions to come. It requires keen observation, a key tool for poets.

Sánchez observes the world from a new perspective, shaped by the sounds of the Americas and condensed into a single vision. This is how the world was meant to be seen: an open field shaped by generations of processes—human, cosmic, and geologic. The observations are then translated into sounds, into syllables that particulate and constellate, experienced by readers as poems in this volume. Poetry is never supposed to be just read; it's supposed to be experienced. A theater. A performance. Language in a dance with torque and skin, bark and scale, root and stem, bloom and tongue. The *z* and *m* and *o* in this collection dance to the tune of breathing and humming bodies.

Language becomes metaphysical in this collection. Like gravity, it transcends space and time and takes form in the way hearts break. The characters in this collection are both human and non-human, all alive just the same thanks to the language used within the book. Sparrowhawks become brothers because the syllables invite them to do so—a simple turn toward a future of relation and intention. Language is both dream and the everyday in this collection. Like the air we breathe, it journeys from chest to leaf and back again, filtering through the memories of itself: dandelion seeds and fireflies floating through summer evenings. This collection reminds us that we see the same evenings and experience chrysanthemums the same. Language offers us this experience, and the poem is the site of language, alive and dancing as if a body in a living room or kitchen, a bird diving into a flowing river, children walking along a border. Here is a universal language, a "universe's language" as written in the poem "Aj' jara'is tzi'upä' / Mi padre me dio un regalo / My Father Gave Me a Gift." In this poem, and throughout the entire collection, we are given many gifts, and these gifts teach us how to sing:

> We are men and women of our word.
> There in the mountains the wewe grows,
> a yellow flower with orange spots,
> a bird that sings
> and teaches the Zoques to sing
> we, we, we
> ore, ore, ore
> wik, wik, wik.

So let the story of this book river through you the way oxygen does because it is a gift. A gift of journey, hope, and plight. *How to Be a Good Savage and Other Poems* is an almanac for a future that is possible if we begin to trace the way words have spark, syllable, and sparrows. They try every day to gift us something. We just need to listen to them, hear them rattle or sing in the trees, from the volcanoes, along the ocean. Start here, read these poems, hear them sing.

JAKE SKEETS, 2023

Note on the Translations

How to Be a Good Savage and Other Poems draws from Mikeas Sánchez's six published collections. All were originally published in bilingual Zoque-Spanish editions between 2006 and 2019, five in Mexico and one in Puerto Rico, the first when Sánchez was twenty-seven. She drafted her earliest poems, those in *Tumjama maka mujsi' / Y sabrás un día* (And One Day You Will Know), in Spanish, the language of her formal education, and later rendered them in Zoque. Subsequent works were either composed simultaneously in both languages or fully composed in Zoque and then self-translated into Spanish. Like most bilingual Indigenous poets in Mexico, Sánchez translates her own Zoque poems into Spanish because of the dearth of Zoque-Spanish literary translators. Even the standardization of Zoque as a written language remains in process. Indeed, Sánchez's body of literature has played a significant role in that standardization. This volume is the first published in any country to update the Zoque orthography of her earlier poems to reflect the most current conventions.

By the time Sánchez published her second book, *Mumure' nhtä' yäjktampä / Todos somos cimarrones* (We're All Maroons), she had begun composing her poetry simultaneously in both Zoque and Spanish. Many of the poems in this book are set in Barcelona, Spain, where she earned a master's in language education as a Ford Foundation fellow. These poems draw comparisons between the lives of the African migrants she encountered in Spain and Indigenous Latin American migrants in the United States. While at first glance the book's title might seem metaphorical, or perhaps hyperbolic, over 200,000 enslaved Africans had been forcibly transported to Mexico by 1829, when the institution of slavery was formally abolished there. Much of Chiapas' Indigenous population was trapped in peonage until the early twentieth century. Sánchez's own ancestors—as recently as her great-grandparents—were forced into labor at the hacienda in her home community, Ajway. In a powerful reversal, the buildings of that old hacienda now serve as the first (and only) high school in Ajway—where Sánchez's daughter studies.

Because of their subject matter, which often speaks to the universality of displacement and oppression of the marginalized, and setting, whether in Barcelona or New York City, Sánchez calls the poems from *We're All Maroons* (2012) her "non-Indigenous poems." As she explains, "At that time only writing about certain themes was considered Indigenous literature." Sánchez's work has helped subvert that idea. One thread running through her body of work is an insistence on women's voices in all matters of political, spiritual, artistic, and intellectual life. This, too, is part of her poetry's subversive power. As she explains, in traditional Zoque culture "all activities related to wisdom are assigned to men. Women can't participate."

For the last decade, which includes the publication of her books *Mojk'jäyä / Mokaya* (Mokaya, 2013) and *Jujtzye tä wäpä tzamapänh'ajä / Cómo ser un buen salvaje* (How to Be a Good Savage, 2019), Sánchez has written her poems first in Zoque, then rendered them in Spanish. The process of self-translation served an editorial function as well, as it often demanded that she tinker with one version or the other until she felt fully satisfied with both. As Zoque assumed primacy, her poems began to feature

Zoque cosmology, history, and myth more directly. Earlier poems refer to common Zoque beliefs about, for example, the ominous mushrooms and black moths whose appearance portends death. Her later poems explicitly foreground Zoque cosmology, with frequent appearances of key deities like Pyokpatzyuwe, the Goddess of Time, and of El Chichón, the volcano that rises over Ajway. El Chichón, known as Tzitzunhgätzüjk in Zoque, has indelibly marked every aspect of life in Sánchez's home community. It erupted in 1982, when Sánchez was a baby. Nine Zoque villages were destroyed and nearly two thousand people lost their lives. It was the deadliest natural disaster of the twentieth century in Mexico. The eruption left Sánchez's family homeless. They moved to the town of Ajway and built the house where her mother and one of her sisters still live. Sánchez lives next door. In day-to-day conversation, Ajway residents still locate events in time by noting whether they were "before" or "after," referring to the 1982 eruption.

Translating from two parallel but distinct versions of a single poem poses unique challenges—primarily, which version to prioritize when they diverge more than the single English version can bear—as well as opportunities for insight into how each language works to achieve the poet's intended effect. We devoted significant time to deciding how to render the Zoque names of gods, deities, and ancestors. In many of her Spanish-language poems, Sánchez chose to leave the names in Zoque, often including explanatory footnotes. For this trilingual edition, the three of us decided to eliminate those footnotes and incorporate that information into endnotes. Sánchez explains that she sometimes retained the Zoque name simply because she couldn't find a Spanish translation that pleased her. In other cases, she specifically wanted the Zoque name in the Spanish version of the poem. As she says, "We want to bring a bit of this world to English readers so that they might understand it. We want to share a few of our most important [entities] with them."

The three of us chose to begin this volume with poems from Sánchez's 2013 collection *Mojk'jäyä / Mokaya*, as they help ground readers in Zoque cosmology and belief systems as well as Sánchez's feminist poetic voice. Selections from the other books appear in the order in which they were published. These poems show us Sánchez's creative development over fifteen years, as she studies in Spain, where her daughter was born; returns to Mexico, lives in the city as a single parent and works as a bilingual Zoque-Spanish radio producer; and then moves back to her community in Ajway to (thus far successfully) fight against various industrial development pressures—including oil fracking.

Zoque forms one branch of the larger Mixe-Zoquean family of Indigenous languages of southern Mexico. According to the Mexican government's 2020 language census, there are just over 110,000 speakers across seven Zoque languages, several of which are not mutually intelligible. The Zoque people have sustained their language in spite of nearly five centuries of genocidal policies, which is a triumph. Sánchez writes in the Copainalá variant of Chiapas Zoque—though she often uses words from other Zoque variants in her poems. Copainalá Zoque has an estimated 15,000 speakers and is considered endangered due to a rapid language shift to Spanish. While rich in oral tradition, Zoque has not commonly been used as a medium for written literature. Sánchez stands out as both a trailblazer in that emerging tradition—as the first woman to publish a book of poetry in her language—and as a champion of protecting, preserving, and strengthening the Zoque language. As Sánchez explains, "To be an Indigenous writer in Mexico is an act of protest, an act of cultural and linguistic resistance, and also a battle against the Mexican educational system and against Mexico's literary elites."

In addition to Sánchez's vocation as a poet, she worked for seven years as a radio producer for the multilingual radio station XECOPA, which broadcasts in both Zoque and Tsotsil alongside Spanish, playing an important role in the continued use and mainstream visibility of those Indigenous languages. She currently works as a Zoque-Spanish translator and developer of Zoque-language curricula for elementary schools. Sánchez weaves together poetry and activism in every aspect of her creative and community life. She is a cofounder of ZODEVITE, a Zoque land-defense organization. The name is an acronym for the group's full name in Spanish, which translates as Faith-Based Zoque Community Defending Life and Earth. ZODEVITE is, against all odds, successfully opposing mining, oil fracking, hydroelectric damming, and other large-scale threats to traditional Zoque lands. Some of Sánchez's poems, including several in this volume, serve as antifracking anthems in Chiapas and elsewhere, appearing on banners at marches and on the walls of village buildings. In 2017, ZODEVITE won the Pax Christi International Peace Prize, the first time a Mexican organization had received this award. Sánchez was chosen by ZODEVITE as their representative to accept the prize in Rome.

We have been fortunate to count Mikeas as a close—and essential—collaborator in the translation of this book. As neither of us speaks or reads Zoque, we relied on Sánchez's own Spanish versions to make our initial translations. We later worked closely with the poet herself to understand how the two versions of each poem diverge, and why. In most instances, we have prioritized the Zoque original over the Spanish version. To give just one example: in the poem "We Are Mokayas," the final line in the Spanish poem reads "we will give you the secret to infinite beauty," while the Zoque reads "secret to infinite wisdom." In English, we chose "secret to the sublime."

We began working together on this book in 2020. Shook had previously translated most of the poems that appear here from Sánchez's first four books as well as the first three poems from *Mojk'jäyä / Mokaya*. Wendy translated several additional early poems, the other twenty-two poems from that 2013 book, and the poems from Sánchez's most recent (2019) collection, *Jujtzyi'e nhtä wäpä tzamapänh'ajä / Cómo ser un buen salvaje*. Our translation process entailed several rounds of passing the poems back and forth, to revise and polish them. Our goal was to ensure that Sánchez's voice rang true in English, even as our translations chart her evolution as a poet. In October 2021, after our plans to visit Sánchez in Ajway were cancelled by the pandemic, the three of us met in Oaxaca City to review and discuss our translations. We reviewed each poem line by line, observing the differences between the Zoque and Spanish versions. During those two days, several video calls, and countless emails and messages, Sánchez offered us an intensive education in Ajway history, culture, language, and belief systems—all with endless generosity and patience. Sánchez also recorded the Zoque originals in her voice, helping us bring some measure of the orality of the original into the English. In October 2022, as we finalized this collection, Wendy was able to visit Ajway briefly, to see and hear and experience the place where many of these poems were born.

Sánchez says of her chosen mode of expression, "Not only is poetry important for sharing and understanding our people's beliefs, it is also important as an act of resistance, to denounce all the injustices that we are subjected to as Indigenous peoples." She believes her poetry comes not from herself alone, but from the Zoque community as a whole.

She refers to the words—*te'tzameram* or *las palabras*—of her poems as the "sole inheritance of [her] lineage" in the fifth poem that appears in this book. References to "la palabra" appear over and over in her poems. "The word" has religious overtones—as it does in English—but it can also refer to all knowledge, the sacred path, or one's reason for being. As Sánchez says, "I think this poetry is also a type of spell. It is a way to invoke our ancestors and be born again with them." We are grateful that Sánchez has chosen to share her words with us and with you.

WENDY CALL AND SHOOK

ORE'YOMO

TUMÄ

Xky'a'e
mij' jara'is syupana' jaya'une
ji'na myusi'ankäna' jujtzyi'e' mij' jonhtzyi'wane'jinh
Makana' mpämipäjki'a'e' ore'päntam
maka'na tzapwiru'ya'e ore'yomo'ram
Syka'e ja' syutyaä'pä
yajk' myijkspapäis te' sawa' mapasyiä'piak'
nhkya'e jonhtzyi'kojama
Syki'a'e tuj'sawa'kojama
Nhkya'e natzkuy'jinh pänajupä
käwänhpapä myayis'pyayukämä'
kätyajpasenh'omo joyjo'yeram
ponyi'ponyi
Sykya'e kosyi'tyaksipä
popya'wyjtpapä apyjt'omoram
ji' jyamepäis' toya
Nhkya'e pänajupä' tuj'anhsänh'omo
mij' nhkojama' ejsi're

ORE'YOMO

UNO

Niña
tu padre prefirió niño
porque no sabía que con tu canto
   de alondra
renacería el poder de los ore'pät
la voz antigua de las ore'yomo
Niña no deseada
aquella que sacude el viento mientras sueña
nkiae espíritu ave
syka'e espíritu tormenta
Niña parida con miedo
aquella que se esconde bajo el manto de su
   madre
mientras los duendes pasan despacio
sin prisa
Niña pies descalzos
aquella que corre entre las zarzas
y no hay dolor que se le resista
Niña nacida en tiempo de lluvia
tu nagual es un cangrejo

ORE'YOMO

ONE

Girl
your father wanted a boy
because he didn't know what to do with your
   lark's song
the power of the ore'pät will be reborn
the ancient voice of the ore'yomo
Unwanted girl
stirring the wind with her dreams
nkiae spirit bird
syka'e spirit storm
Girl born fearful
who hides beneath her mother's shawl
while duendes stroll slowly by
unhurried
Girl running barefoot
through the brambles
there is no pain that can defeat her
Girl born during rainy season
a crab is your nagual

METZA'

Papinyi'omo
jäyä'mayu
jäyä'une
sänhkä'
jomepä'yomo
Papinyi'omo nhkäwänhpapä'is mij' nhteksi'kämä
omyajpapä' musoki'uy
Papinyomo' nhjyä'pyapä'is
ji' nhkomusi'anhkä mij' winapä'ijtku'y
Yom'komi anhuku'is'nyeram
papinyi'omo'
minä' wanä' äjtzyinh,
minä' ma nhtä' jampärame' nhtä' nhtoya'ram
yä' apijt' tä' taj'tampapä'is
mina' tzätzä'
mina' ma' nhtä'' yatzyi'ä'tyame'
mumu' te' tzuj'yajupä' nhtä'
näyi'käsiram

DOS	TWO
Muchacha	Young woman
flor de mayo	May flower
capullo	chrysalis
resplandor	resplendence
vientre en plenilunio	full-moon belly
Muchacha que escondes bajo tu falda	Young woman who hides
los secretos más exquisitos	exquisite secrets beneath her skirt
Muchacha que lloras	Young woman who cries
porque desconoces tu origen	for not knowing her roots
Diosa milenaria	Ancient goddess
muchacha	young woman
ven a cantar conmigo	come sing with me
ven a olvidar esto que nos hiere	come forget what wounds us
esta espinita que se nos encarna	this thorn that pierces us
ven hermana mía	come my sister
ven a maldecir conmigo	come with me to join our voices
a todos aquellos que escupieron sobre	against any who spit on
nuestro origen	our roots

TUKAY

Nhtzu'mayi'
Oko'tzyuwe
Nhtä' natzpapä'tzyuwe
pyeka'tzuwe
yijspäjk'papäis wäpä'tiyä ji' wyapä' tiyä
Sutkuyis' myama, toya'is'myama
jyampä'yajupä yom'nhkomi
pämi'äyupä' nhkomi
yajk' tu'pi'apäis te' juktäjk, jyapä'pyapä'is te'
matza'ram
Nhtzu'mayi'
jene'watpapä
sunyi'ejtzpabä
kasäjpa kowa'najkspapä
Kotzäjkis'myama
motzyi'rampä' kopänh'is nhkyomi'
kyoke'tyi'ajpapäis mäjarampä' kopänh
tanäs'myamaram
punus'tzyi'ätzäram
Nhtä" jameminä' makak'käjtzi' mij' nhtu'ni'

Abuela
Oko'tzyuwe
Anciana temible
mujer antigua
conocedora del bien y del mal
Madre del placer y del dolor
diosa renegada
poderosa deidad
que apagas el fuego y enciendes las
estrellas
Abuela
la más cantora
la más danzante
la más tambora
Virgen del inframundo
dueña de los animales pequeños
protectora de las bestias feroces
madre de las plantas
hermana de los peces
Acuérdate de mí cuando llegue a tu casa

Grandmother
Oko'tzyuwe
Fearsome
old woman
knower of right and of wrong
Mother of pleasure and of pain
renegade Goddess
powerful deity
who snuffs out the fire and ignites the
stars
Grandmother
best singer
best dancer
best drummer
Virgin of the inner world
master of small animals
protector of ferocious beasts
mother of plants
sister of fish
Remember me when I arrive

WEJPÄJ'KI'UY

TUMÄ

Nasakopajk' nhtyajk' pajkapi'apäis' äj' nhtoya
nhtyajk' pajkapi'apäis äj' nhkiskuy teserike äj' natzkuy
nhtä' nhkomi' naptzu'isnyi'e
tzayi'isnyi'e teserike' pitzä'isnyi'e
mij' me'tzapyatzi mij' nhtzama'omoma
mij' nhkosanhtäjk totzyi'äjkupä'
äj' une'ijtkuy'omo
Äjtzi'
mij' metz'patzi tumtu'mäpä tzyina' kujyomo
jurä' tzäyaju' äj' nhkasäj'ki'utyam
Äjtzi'
mij' metzapyatzi mij' kartenya'jäyä'oma mij' kapulinh'oma
mij' nhtuk'tam takyajpapä mapa'syiäpyasenh'omo

NOMBRAR LAS COSAS

UNO

Oh Nasakopajk' que aplacas mi amargura
que acallas mi ira y mi
    espanto
oh Dios de la mañana
de la tarde y de la noche
persigo tu olor a selva alta
tus pasos de bestia herida
corriendo por mi infancia
Un trozo de mí
te busca en cada árbol de naranjo
donde quedó colgada mi alegría
Un trozo de mí
evoca tu sabor a gardenia y
    capulín
tus senderos que se bifurcan mientras
    sueño

TO NAME THINGS

ONE

Oh Nasakopajk' may you ease my
    bitterness
quiet my shock and
    rage
oh God of morning
of afternoon and evening
I trace your rainforest scent
a wounded animal's footsteps
wandering through my childhood
Part of me
seeks you in every orange tree
where my happiness hangs
Part of me
conjures your gardenia and
    wild cherry flavor
your pathways diverging in my
    dreams

METZA

Wäkä' yajk'pajka'yaä' äj' anima'is kyänhtätzä'ram
yajk' mina' yäki' te' moki'omoma'
te' almenhtras'yomoma
te' yokapä' violinh'is wyane'
te' wäpyä' yetze' tzunh'tyis'nyi'e
Nasakopajk' nhtä' mpäjkinh'nhtzyonh'ja äj' nhkonuks'kuy
mij' aknyi'amä' te' wenhti'ram
jyamopyamä' te' ya'tzyiä'kyutyam
Tzamas'jyara'
jajtzyuku'is'kyowina', kak'is'kyowina'
akuakä' te' Ipstäjk'

DOS

Para calmar la sed de mis muertos
venga aquí el olor de la pimienta
el sabor de la almendra
la nota más cálida del violín
la danza más fecunda del sembrador
Oh Nasakopajk', recibe con agrado mis
   plegarias
del lado izquierdo las ofrendas
del lado derecho las injurias
Oh dueño del monte
amo de las hormigas y de los tigres
abre los cerrojos del Ipstäjk

TWO

To quench my ancestors' thirst
I summon the scent of black pepper
the taste of almond
the violin's warmest note
the sower's most fertile dance
Oh Nasakopajk', please hear my prayers
my offerings on the left
my misdeeds on the right
Oh mountain guardian
king of jaguars and ants
open the locks of Ipstäjk

TUKAY

Tekoroya mitu'tzi mij' nhtziya'e' äj' nhzame'ram Yasyi'palanki
yä' tzajkayajupä' äj anhuku'istam
mitutzi' mij' wajne yä' wane' muspäjkupätzi äj' mama'is tzyejk'omo
Tzu'anhnak äj' nhtäjk
Jiksek' ispäjk'pajna' mij' winujpajk'
muspajna' mij' nhkänu'ka mij' näyi'
Jiksek äj nhkojamarena konukskuy'täjk'
tujkupä tu'räjinh, toto'jäyäjinh
Jiksek äjtejna' tumä' masanh'täjk' moki'ompapä
Tekoroya mitutzi mij' nhtziya'e' äj' nhzame'ram Yasyi'palanki
yä' musoki'uy' tziyajupätzi' äj' mapasyi''omo

TRES

Por eso vine Yasyi'palanki, a ofrendarte
   mis palabras
única herencia de mi linaje
vine a cantarte esta canción que aprendí
   desde el vientre de mi madre
cuando mi casa aún era el Tzu'anh'
Yo entonces reconocía tu rostro lo mismo
   que los senderos
para llegar a tu nombre
Yo entonces tenía un altar de palmas y
   bugambilias
en el centro de mi alma
Yo entonces era un templo oloroso a
   pimienta
Por eso vine Yasyi'palanki a ofrendarte mis
   palabras
único don que se me ha revelado en sueños

THREE

I have come, Yasyi'palanki, to offer you my
   words
the sole inheritance of my lineage
I have come to sing you this song learned
   in the womb
when I still lived in Paradise
I recognized your face like I did the path
that led me to your unspoken name
And so I kept an altar of palm and
   bougainvillea
at the center of my soul
And so I was a pepper-scented temple
That is why I came, Yasyi'palanki, to offer
   you my words
my sole talent revealed to me in dreams

MAJKSYI'KUY

Äjte'na te' yomo'
ejtzpapä kujkmä
pojk'tzyi'unhpapä' äj' asa'jinh
Sawapät'is myusoki'uy'jinh
Äjte'na te' nijpapä'yomo
te' mä'a'is'myama te' näjtzis'myama
Äjtzi' te oko'chuwe
nhtya'tzyiä'yajpapäis' yaknakajse'
te' nhkäwänyi'ajupä' nhtä' nhkomiram

CUATRO

Yo también fui la danzante
que bailaba en medio de la plaza
con mi túnica al viento
y los secretos de Sawapät' en la lengua
Yo la sembradora
la madre del venado y del armadillo
Yo la oko'chuwe
que blasfemaba con mayor fervor
a los dioses escondidos

FOUR

I too was the dancer
who whirled in the plaza
the Wind Lord's breeze in my tunic
and Sawapät's secrets on my tongue
I the sower
mother of deer and armadillos
I the ancient grandmother Oko'chuwe
who blasphemed with zeal
our hidden gods

MOJSAY

Kasujpa’ yajk’täjkä te’ jomepä’ ejtztayu’
tzyi’ap’tziyajum’ te’ musoki’uy
wyäjä’tziyajum te’ jäyä’ram
tyu’nyi’ajum’ myapasyio’omo
nhkyopinh’jayajum nhkyojama sik’tyinh’tzokopyä
Yäti’ makam’ mawe’ mumupä’ sunh’omoram
yisanh’tziyajum’ te’ tzame
pyomitzi’um Sawa’pänis
yajk’ kätum’ Toki’is
Kasujpa’ yajk’täjkä te’ jomepä’ ejtztayu’

CINCO

Bienvenido el nuevo danzante
ya le fue revelado el secreto
ya tuvo el regalo de las flores
fue visitado su sueño
fue ungido su nagual corazón de cigarra
Ahora estará en todas las fiestas
le fue mostrada la palabra
le ha dado poder el Señor del viento
le ha dado licencia el Señor del fuego
Bienvenido el nuevo danzante

FIVE

Welcome new dancer
to whom the secret has been revealed
who has been anointed
with flowers in a dream
with the cicada-nagual's song
Now he will be at every festival
having crossed the threshold to the sacred
    word
he holds the Wind Lord's power
he has received the Fire King's seal
Welcome new dancer

TUJTAY

Poksupä' mäja'pijstinh'kämä
peka'kujy nhkotzonh'opyapä
te' Nhtzunh'tyi'is yajk' tupya'tzyame
nhtä' nhkomis' tzyajmapya nhkyowi'kämä
te' wejpäjkuyis' tzyame'
punus'tzyame'ram
tanäs'tzyame'ram
Motzyi'rampä' kopänis'tzyameram
Poksupä' mäja'pistinh'kämä
nhtä' nhkomi' ona're jäyäjse' ketpapä
yampapäis te' tzayi'
anhkamupä' wyränh'jinh'tam

Sentado bajo la ceiba más colosal
árbol protector de voces antiguas
el sembrador apaga su silencio
Ahí Dios susurra a su oído
esa palabra invocada
lenguaje secreto de los peces
las plantas
y los animales pequeños
Sentado bajo la ceiba más colosal
Dios es una nube en forma de flor
contemplando el atardecer
con los ojos vendados

Seated under the tallest ceiba
guardian-tree of ancient voices
the Great Sower kindles his silence
There God whispers in his ear
those sacred words
secret language of fishes
of plants
of small creatures
Seated under the giant ceiba
God is a flower-shaped cloud
observing the sunset
with blinded eyes

KUYAY

Ijtu jyama aku'ajpak te' Tzu'anh
wäkä tä' tzajmatyamä mumu ti'is yijtku'y
tumä popyapä tzame
tumä kene' mapasyis'nyi'e
Te' Tzu'anh
nhtä' anhuku'is tzajkatya'upä kojama
te' tuwis' wyränh'tit wäkä nhtä' a'myaä kayajupä
Tese' mumu' ti'is ijtu' kyomusjkuy
te' tzame ji' nhtä nhkämetzepä
ji' wyäpä tä' mujsä tzame
mumä pänis'
mumu yomo'is
wenenh'omo myetzyajpa te' tzame ji' kyomusyi'a'epä

SIETE

Hay días en que el Tzu'anh se abre
para revelarnos el origen de las cosas
una línea de fuga
una imagen que se nos escapa del letargo
El Tzu'anh
nuestra herencia de nagual
nuestra lagaña de perro para mirar los
    muertos
Porque todo tiene su enigma
su razón innecesaria
su motivo sobrante
Todo hombre
toda mujer
algún día buscan esa palabra que les falta

SEVEN

Some days Tzu'anh opens up
revealing to us the origin of all life
the known world's limits
an image escaping from our dreams
Tzu'anh
shelters our nagual birthright
our dog's tears so we can see the dead
Because everything has its mystery
its needless reason
its special motive
Every man
every woman
will one day seek the wisdom they need

TUKURUJTAY

Tese' nukpa jyama
wäkä wyanh'nhtyotza te' jome' nisujopyapä'
yäti' maka' nyiäj'maya'e yatz'pät
yäti' maka' nyiäj'maya'e nhtzuj'kopya'
Mama 'Karmen pyopo'asa'jinh
mitum tzujsnu'pajk'omopä
jäyä'mayu'jinh'tam
Pyokpatzyuwe
watum' myapasyi'omo
ejtzum kyojama'jinh
Yäti' maka' yispäki te' peka'tzame
yäti' maka' myapa'syiäyi te' tzama'komi
yäti' maka' 'yise wynäjpajk anhsänh'yomo kowinas'nyi'e

OCHO

Así de pronto llega el día
y el curandero debe cantar con su voz de
   pulsador
ahora será el nigromante
ahora lo llamarán hechicero
La Virgen del Carmen vestida de blanco
ha salido del Tzujsnu'pajk
con un ramillete de flores de mayo
Pyokpatzyuwe
ha cantado en el centro de su sueño
ha bailado con su nagual
Ahora conocerá la palabra antigua
ahora soñará con el dueño del monte
ahora mirará de frente a la señora del tiempo

EIGHT

So quickly comes the day
and the curandero must sing with his
   healer's voice
now he'll be the necromancer
now they'll call him conjurer
The Virgin of Carmen dressed in white
has given mountain guardian Tzujsnu'pajk
a bouquet of mayflowers
Pyokpatzyuwe
has sung in his dreams
has danced with his nagual
Now he will learn the ancient word
now he will dream of the mountain guardian
now he will face the goddess of time

MAJKUSTUJTAY

Yäre' te' masanh'jama sustayus'nyi'e
yäti' maka' yispäjke yanhuku'is nyiäpinh_
yäti' maka' nyiä' mejtzanh'kanh'e 'myä'a'kojama
Maka' tzyake jyara', myama
nhtyomo, yune'ram
wäkä' tyumä'ajä' sawas'wyanejinh
Yäti' jinam ma' nyiäjmaya'e jaya'une
jinam' ma' nyiäjmaya'e närunh u jara'
maka' nyiäjma'ya'e sustayu'
yispäjkpapä'is katzi'is wyane
kyoketpapäis te' anhsänh
muspapä' nhwyrä' mapasyi'omo

NUEVE

Este es el día sagrado del pitero
hoy conocerá la memoria de su sangre
hoy caminará lado a lado con su nagual
   venado
Y dejará a su padre y a su madre
y a su esposa y a sus hijos
para enlazarse con la eufonía del viento
Ahora ya no será llamado hijo
ni esposo ni padre
sino pitero
conocedor del lenguaje del tucán
medidor del tiempo
el que tiene la llave para caminar en los
   sueños

NINE

This is the flute player's sacred day
today he will meet blood memory
today his deer nagual will accompany him
He will leave his father and mother
and wife and children
to meld with the wind's sweet sound
He will no longer be called son
nor husband nor father
but flautist
speaker of the toucan's language
marker of time
holder of the key to enter our dreams

MAJKAY

Misyi'u' kotzäj'käjsi
sirijtum' te' kowarayu'
yajk' kätum' te Tokis'
yajk' täjkäyum te' Pyokpatzyuwe'is
Nyi'ajksum nhkyowa' te' peka'tyapa
temä te' kokonä'mä
Yäki' te' konukskuy wäkä' tyajk' pakä' te' kiskuy
Wäkä' nhtä' majkpä'ya'ä te' natzkutyam
Yäki' te' mä'a'is nyi'aka wäkä nhtä' mona' te' kowa'
yäki' te tzajy wäkä' nhtä warä' te' topyapä' nhtä' jame'

En la cúspide más alta del Misyiu'kotzäjk
el tamborero emprendió el vuelo
le ha dado permiso el Señor del fuego
le ha dado licencia la Diosa del volcán
Ha tocado su primera nota en la vieja Teapan
en la gruta del Kokonä
Aquí el centro ceremonial para acallar la ira
y ceñir el espanto
Aquí la piel del venado para cubrir el
    cuerpo del tambor
aquí el hilo de ixtle para amarrar la
    doliente memoria

On Misyiu'kotzäjk's highest peak
the drummer took flight
the Fire King has given him permission
the Volcano Goddess has empowered him
He has drummed the first beat in old Teapa
in the Kokonä cave
Here in the ceremonial center to soothe rage
and cast out espanto
Here's the deerskin to cover the drum's body
here's the ixtle cord to bind aching memory

MOJK'JÄYÄ

Wanjampatzi te' sis' teserike te sutku'y
[. . .] tese' mumu'tiyä, mumu tzyi'ä'tyiä'tyampä tiyä' äj nepa'
tä' komiste' tzyäki.

—WALT WHITMAN

TUMÄ

Yomo'tzyiä
tese' anhkasäpyatzi äj' nhwyt
tumtumäpä' tzäki'tzäki tujkupä'jinh
anhkasäpyatzi äj' natz'kutyam, äj' nhkasäjkyu'tyam
Mumurampä kipsoki'uy
wurampäre' äjne'ankä'ram
Yomo'tzyiä tese' anhkasäpyatzi tumtumäpä äj'näpinh'tzajy
juwä' ijtyaju wänyi'ajupä äj' anhuku'is myusoki'utyam
tese' mumurämpä tzame' ore'pänis'nyi'eram ijtyaju äj' aknakomo
tese' mumurämpa kokypskuy ore'yomos'nyi'eram ijtyi'aju äj' tzujomo'

MOKAYA

Creo en la carne y en los apetitos,
[. . .] y cada parte, cada pizca de mí
es un milagro

—WALT WHITMAN

UNO

Soy mujer
y celebro cada pliegue de mi cuerpo
cada minúsculo átomo que me forma
y donde navegan mis dudas y mis
    esperanzas
Todas las contradicciones son maravillosas
porque me pertenecen
Soy mujer y celebro cada arteria
donde aprisiono los secretos de mi estirpe
y todas las palabras de los ore'pät están en
    mi boca
y toda la sabiduría de las ore'yomo están en
    mi saliva

MOKAYA

I believe in the flesh and the appetites,
[. . .] and each part and tag of me
is a miracle

—WALT WHITMAN

ONE

I am woman
and I celebrate every crease of my body
each tiny atom that composes me
where my hopes and doubts flow
All my contradictions are marvelous
because they are mine
I am woman and I celebrate every vein
where I guard my ancestors' secrets
every Zoque man's word in my mouth
every Zoque woman's wisdom in my spit

METZA

Tzampatzi' toya'isyi'ajpapä nhki'a'e'is' nyi'oyikäsiram
te' mäjtzä'yajpapä' natze'jinh
pitzä'runh'omo
Tekoroya'ram winapä' mayo'poyas'tyi'uj
te' wejkä' paru'wisnyi'e
Tekoroya'ram yomkak'is' 'wyejkä
jäyäs'yomaram
Yajk' mytyi'aä te' kumunu teserike te' tajpi'ram
yajk' masanäj'ya'yaä' nkya'e'is' tyoya'ram
topyapä tzotzusenh'omo nasakopajk
Yajk' mytyi'aä Pyokpatzyi'uwe teserike Kopajktzoka'
yajk' isanh'sajyaä kotzäjkis syi'asa'ajkuy

Me nombro y hablo por todas las niñas
   maltratadas
que juegan su inocencia
desde un callejón sin farolas
Para ellas la primera lluvia de mayo
y el rugido del lobo
Para ellas el gemido de la tigresa
y el olor a madreselva de la ternura
Que vengan la codorniz y el gavilán
a ungir el alma de todas estas niñas heridas
desde la memoria primigenia del hombre
Que vengan Pyokpatzyi'uwe y Kopajktzoka'
a mostrar la belleza del inframundo

I name myself and speak for all the
   mistreated girls
who gamble their innocence
in a darkened alley
For them May's first rain
and the wolf's roar
For them the tigress's howl
and the honeysuckle scent of tenderness
May brother sparrowhawk and sister quail
soothe the souls of all the girls wounded
since the beginning of human time
May Pyokpatzyi'uwe and Kopajktzoka' come
to show us the beauty of the great beyond

TUKAY

Tzampatzi' nyi'ujkyaräjupä' papinyi'omos' nyi'äyi'käsiram
myet'tzyajpapäis nhwyt ojkjä'ä'is wyejkä'omo
kokokujyis' myjks'kä'omo
Tzampatzi' yom'kotzäjkis' nyiäyi'käjsi
Tzitzunh'kotzäjk
tzampatzi' jaya'kotzäjkis' nyiäyi' käjsi
Jakima'kotzäjk
kejyaj'papä masanh' 'nenh'a'käjsi

Tzampatzi' kojamas'nyi'äyikäjsi
teyi' juwä ji' tä känuki najs'toya'is
Tzampatzi' te' masahn' yom'ijtkuyis' nyi'äyi'käjsi
'syka'e'is 'nyiäyi'käsi'ram
te' nhkya'e' ji' nyi'atzya'epä'is toya
sirij'tyajpapä mäja' jonhtzyij'se
wäkä' yisanh'sajyaä käsipä' 'mpyämi
Ja' yajk' komuj'syi'a'äpä' kätupä' anhsänh'omo

Me nombro y hablo por todas las
   muchachas violadas
que buscan su niñez en el zumbido del
   abejorro
y en el vaivén de la palmera
Hablo en nombre del cerro hembra
Tzitzunh'kotzäjk
y del cerro macho
Jakima'kojtzäjk
que se yerguen poderosos en la llanura
   sagrada

Hablo del alma
cuya inmortalidad no alcanzan el oprobio
   ni la duda
Hablo del sexo inmaculado
de las niñas perennes
que se alzan por encima del desconsuelo
como águila y cóndor
mostrando su grandeza
doblegada por el paso de los tiempos

I name myself and speak for all the raped
   girls
who seek their childhood in a bumblebee's
   buzz
and in a palm tree's sway
I speak in the name of the female volcano
Tzitzunh'kotzäjk
and the male mountain
Jakima'kojtzäjk
who rise mightily from the sacred plain

I speak of the soul
its immortality untouchable by shame or
   doubt
I speak of blessed purity
of the perennial girls
who soar above their grief
like the condor and eagle
whose magnificence hides
under the passing years

MAJKSYKUY

Nhkotzampatzi äj' mayi'
yajk' äkpapä'is nhkyojama' Pyokpatzyuwe'is'pyayu'kämä
täjp'wyjtpapä tzawijse' myotzyi'une'ijtkuy'omo
sojkuy'kämäram
Nhkyps'patzi' äj' mayi'omo
jä'ä te'omo nhkyps'patzi'
nhkyps'patzi' nhkyastanyi'a'oma'omo
te' wänupä jyotzkuy'omo
ji' musipä' nhtä' nhkätäj'käjya
Nhkyps'patzi äj' mayi'omo
tese' te'is nhkyps'pa not'papä'jyara'omo
jyokpapäis te' mampasawa' kyotzampapäis te' tuj'
jyokpapäis yijsä' jojpajk'omo nikurakapä äj' matzyuwe
ipskotumäpä'yame'jinh

CUATRO

Hablo de mi madre
cuyo nagual se agazapa bajo el manto de
   Pyokpatzyuwe
mientras su niñez es un saraguato
saltando entre los lienzos de caña
Pienso en mi madre
sí pienso en ella
y en su olor a castañas desde la cocina
en esa su ternura casi ciega
impenetrable
Pienso en mi madre
y ella piensa en su padre alcohólico
que espera el viento del norte en señal de
   lluvia
que espera de nuevo mirar en el río a la
   abuela desnuda
con sus dieciséis años

FOUR

I speak of my mother
whose nagual crouches under
   Pyokpatzyuwe's cloak
while her childhood is a howler monkey
leaping among stands of bamboo
I think of my mother
yes, I think of her
and her chestnut scent from the kitchen
in her nearly blind, inviolable
tenderness
I think of my mother
and she thinks of her alcoholic father
who waits for the northern wind as a sign
   of rain
who again waits to watch my grandmother
   naked at the river
at the age of sixteen

MOJSAY

Nhkotzampatzi äj' nhtzu'mama
jene' sunyi' mujspapäis tyi'ukä kafel'
teserike' nyipä' kartenya'jäyä
Äj' nhtzu'mama jäyä'tzäkipä, petzipä'tyi'eksi'jinh
jenerena' syi'utyajpapä tanhtanh'istam
joy'joye'istam
Te'is jyokpana' te' kanikular
yak'pajkpä' yomos'yasajinh
te'is jyokpana' te' kakuy
nu'sanh'wajkupä' tzyi'utzi'jinh
yerpa'pu'enajse' omyajpapä
Mumu tiyä' yajpak
nhtä' jampak tumä mäja'roya
tza'sepä'toya nhtä' nhtzoko'kyäjsi
tere' te' mampasawa' nhtä' nejnapya'päis te' tuj'
tere' te suskuyis'wyane
tyajk' kasäjpapäis

CINCO

Hablo de mi abuela
aquella de manos ávidas para el corte de
   café
y el cultivo de las gardenias
Mi abuela con su amplia falda florida
siempre fue el lugar predilecto de las
   mariposas
y los duendes
Ella esperando la canícula
con su huipil de viuda
ella esperando la muerte
con sus pechos desnudos
y olorosos a hierbabuena
Cuando todo se desmorona
y tienes un dolor como de alga
como de roca
ella es el viento del norte que te trae la
   lluvia
ella es la nota más alta del carrizo
que te trae de nuevo la palabra alegría

FIVE

I speak of my grandmother
her hands so anxious to harvest coffee
and grow gardenias
My grandmother whose wide, flowered
   skirt
was always the butterflies' and duendes'
   favorite place
Awaiting midsummer
in her mourning dress
awaiting death
with her bare breasts
scented with mint
When everything falls apart
and your grief is lichen
is a rock
she is the northern wind that brings rain
she is the highest note of the reeds' song
that brings back joy

TUJTAY

Tzap'ketaritzi' wärampä'yomos' nyiäyi'käjsiram, manyia'yomos'
  nyiäyikäsiram
ja' yispäjkya'äpäis te' sutkuy
te' yomo' yajk' tuyajupä'is yänhku'kyämä
te' sutkuyis' jyuktäjk
jyokyaj'pasenh'omo'na te' kakuyis'yora
konukspa' platapä'rosari'ujinh
Tzapketaritzi' te' ja' kyo'räjkaya'äpä' papinyi'omos' nyiäyi'käjsiram
te'istam wyänyi'aju mumupä' nhkyskuy 'tyi'eksi'kämäram
myasanh'äyaju yänh'kutyam
wäkä' nitumäpä' pät' jana' mujsä' tzyi'äyä'
tejse' nyi'ä' ijtyaju 'totyi'rampä'jaya'une'ram, 'yom'uneram
nhkyetza'yajupä'is tzyejk'tam
ijtyi'aju'senhomo nasakopajkäjsi

SEIS

Hablo también por todas las vírgenes y
   rameras
que nunca conocieron el amor
aquellas que apagaron bajo su cama
la hoguera del deseo
mientras esperaban la hora de la muerte
con su rosario de plata
Hablo por todas las muchachas perpetuas
que guardaron todo el odio bajo el plisado
   de su falda
haciendo de su cama un santuario
donde ningún hombre quiso guarecerse
y tuvieron hijos ciegos e hijas tuertas
que mordieron sus vientres
hasta el final de sus días

SIX

I also speak for all the virgins and sluts
who never knew love
those who smothered desire's flame
beneath their beds
while they waited for death
with its silver rosary
I speak for all the perpetual girls
who hid so much hatred in their skirt folds
making their bed into a sanctuary
where no man wanted to take shelter
whose blind sons and one-eyed daughters
gnawed their bellies
until the end of their days

KUYAY

Tzampatzi yomos' nyiäyi'käsiram
yajk' toyajpa'päsma nhtyomo'ajku'y
tekoroya'ram jinma' musipäis tzyi'a'pya'ä nitiyä
teserike nhky'sayajpa'päsma te' sutku'y
tekoroya'ram witpä'jayajpatzi äj' nhkojama'
jäyä mayujse'ompapä
tejinh'tam nhkotzäjk'patzi äj' nhtoya teserijke äj' nhkasojkuy

SIETE

Me nombro y hablo por todas las mujeres
que aún se duelen por su sexo
por todas aquellas que todavía callan
y aborrecen la palabra deseo
a ellas ofrezco mi espíritu
perfumado con flores de mayo
con ellas celebro mi dolor y mi gozo

SEVEN

I speak in the name of women
who are still pained by sex
for all who silence themselves
and loathe the word desire
I offer to them my spirit
scented with May flowers
I celebrate with them my pain and pleasure

TUKURUJTAY

Äj' mama'koroya äj' nhtzu'mama'koroya
witpä'jayaj'patzi' moki'ajyis'yomaram
u'kyajumä' nhtä' nhkomi'ram
witpä'jayaj'patzi te' sunyi'kasäjpapä wane' susta'yusnyi'e
jonhtzyi'ajpapä äkpasenh'omo
Tekoroya'ram
japäpyatzi' sunyi'omyajpapä'kujy
wäkä' yomatzi'jaya'ä wyajtyi'am
tzäki' tzyi'ajkupä Kopajktzoka'is
Tekoroya'ram
käsipä'wane kowarayus'ñyi'e
te' peka'konukskuy ejtzpapäs'nyi'e

OCHO

Para mi madre y mi abuela
ofrezco el aroma de las hojas de pimienta
en que durmieron los santos
ofrezco la canción más alegre del pitero
convertido en pájaro mientras sueña
Para ellas
enciendo palos de ocote
que perfumen sus cabellos
herencia oscura de Kopajktzoka
Para ellas
la nota más centella del tambor
y la oración más antigua del danzante

EIGHT

For my mother and grandmother
I offer the scent of black pepper leaves
where the saints rest
I offer the flautist's happiest song
changed into a bird as he dreams
For them
I burn redolent heart pine
to perfume their hair
dark legacy of Kopajktzoka
For them
the drum's brightest note
and the dancer's age-old prayer

MAJKUSTUJTAY

Masanh'äpyatzi te' jama' jujtzyek' äj' pänaju'
jikä' septiempre' tuj'poya jurä te' tzujsnä'pajkis
yajk· mijnayutzi' äj' jame teserike' yajk' tujkutzi yom'une
Pyokpatzyuwes'yanhuku
Kotzäjkis' nhkyomi teserike tzitzuhn'kotzäjkis'nhkyomi
Masänh'äyajpatzi äj' jara' äj' mayi' tzäjkpujtyaju'ankätzi
tejse' ja' pänajätzi nhkirawa'räjk'omo
yäse' tese' oyu'ri nä' ijtkere' mujapä äj' anhkimoki'uy
tumä' tzokoy' jurä' tumä papinyi'omo pämi'päjkpa'na wäkä' yetza'
toya'kujkmäram
Teserike' äj' nhkomis'tam isanh'tziyajutzi jutzyi'e yatzyi'ona'
tumä to'tzyiäj'kupä ore'omo
Teramte' äj' sasa'ajkuy
teramte' äj' ijtkuy
tere' äj' anhkimoki'uy ni'is jihn'musipä ma' yajk'tzunhja

Bendigo el día de mi nacimiento
aquel septiembre lluvioso donde el
    Tzujsnäpajk
desbordó su memoria y me convirtió en
    niña
descendiente de Pyokpatzyuwe
dueña de las montañas y del volcán
    Tzitzunh
Bendigo a mi padre y a mi madre por
    haberme engendrado
pues aunque no nací en cuna de patricios
tuve mi propio reino
aquella fortaleza insomne donde una
    muchacha danzaba
en medio de las tempestades
Y tuve mis propios dioses que me
    enseñaron a blasfemar
en una lengua amordazada y herida
Esas son mis lindezas
esa mi esencia
ese mi trono que jamás nadie habrá de
    usurparme

NINE

I bless the day of my birth
that rainy September when the
    Tzujsnäpajk River
overflowed its memory and made me into
    a girl
descended from Pyokpatzyuwe
guardian of the mountains and Tzitzunh
I bless my father and my mother for
    having engendered me
although I was not born to nobility
I had my own kingdom
that sleepless castle where a young woman
    danced
amid storms
And I had my own gods who taught me to
    curse
in a gagged and wounded tongue
Those are my beauties
my essence
my throne that no one can seize from me

MAKAY

Masanh'äpyatzi äj' nhkakuy'jama
jurä' Nasakopajkis' makatzi' isanh'tzi'i te' tuk
makatzi' tzajme juwäre te' Tzu'anh'
Jinh'äre' makapä' joki'a'e äj' anhuku'istam
sunh'omo
tzitzunh'kotzäjkis yä'sakämä'
Mopajkis' nyi'ä'kämä
Teyi' makari jo'kyajkere' kisayajpapäis
makatzi' punh'tyi'oyae' tza'jinh
wäkä' nyi'äpujtpäya'ä nhkys'kutyam äj' nhkojama'käjsi
teram' näjmayajpatzi Nasakopaj'kistire' muspapä' ma' wajnä'
te' wane'jinh nyiä' makyaräjpamä te' kayajupä'
temä'anhkas te' Ipstäjk'omo

DIEZ

Bendigo también mis funerales
Nasakopajk' ha de venir a enseñarme el
    camino
que me conducirá al Tzu'anh
Ahí donde aguardan todos mis ancestros
celebrando en eterna fiesta
bajo el manto del volcán Chichón
bajo las aguas del Mobak'
Ahí donde aguardan también mis
    enemigos
esperando su turno para lapidarme
para descargar su enemistad contra mi
    alma yerta
pero sólo Nasakopajk' podrá cantar
la marcha fúnebre que me conducirá
por siempre al Ipstäjk'

TEN

I also bless my funeral
Nasakopajk' will come to show me the
    path
that will guide me to Tzu'anh
There where all my ancestors await
celebrating an endless fiesta
under Chichón's skirt
under the waters of the Mobak' River
There where my enemies also stand
waiting their turn to stone me
to sling their hate against my stiff soul
but only Nasakopajk' can sing
the funeral march that will guide me
into the Great Labyrinth for all time

MAJKOTUMÄ

Nhkotzäjk'patzi äj' yom'ijtkuy
teserike' te' sasarampä äj' nunyi'pajk'tam
juwä' kojepa' äj' närunh'
nhkotzäjk'patzi äj' nhkojama'
nhkotzäjk'pajse äj' yom'ijtkuy
Mujstamä' mijtam jujtzyi'e' Nasakopajkis
tzäjka'yajutzi äj' nhtzutzi'ram
sunyi' tzujkayaju' äj' wynäjpajk
äj' nhtzejk'pajk teserike äj' nhkoso'ram

ONCE

Celebro mi sexo
y las exquisitas formas de mis caderas
donde reposa el hombre que amo
Glorifico mi alma
lo mismo que mis labios mayores y
   menores
Porque Nasakopajk' grande y
   misericordioso
forjó mis pechos
Porque no pudieron haber sido mejores mi
   rostro
mi cintura y mis pies

ELEVEN

I celebrate my sex
and the exquisite shape of my hips
where my lover reclines
I glorify my soul
as well as my inner and outer lips
Because Nasakopajk'
forged my breasts
Because my face and my waist and my feet
could not be more perfectly made

MAJKOMETZA

Jinh suni' tzya'pya'ä äj' näyikäjsi
u'yajk näjmayaju' Kopajktzoka
u Elena u Clitemnestra
u Lesbia u Pyokpatzyuwe
jinh' suni' wäkä' nyi'äpya'ä uka' sunyi äj' nunyi'pajk'
uka' wä' äj' nhtzutzi'is myaja'ajkuy
Mij' nhtzama'tyampatzi jujtzyere jinh'mapä' nhkya'e äj' nhkojama
ji' nhyaya'ejse te' pistinh'tam teserike te' kotzäjk'tam
ji' nhkyaya'ejse te' tum'ijtkuy teserike te' jana'tzapkuy
mij' nhtzamatyam'pátzi jujtzyie' äj' ijtkuyis ja' nyiä' irä' yajkuy
ja' nyi'ä' iräjse yajkuy te' pitzä'is teserike te' kakuy'is

DOCE

No quiero que nadie más me nombre
que nadie me llame Kopajktzoka
o Helena o Clitemnestra
o Lesbia o Pyokpatzyuwe
que nadie más diga si le gustan mis caderas
o el tamaño de mis pechos
Porque mi alma es inmortal
lo mismo que la ceiba y los volcanes
lo mismo que la soledad y el silencio
y mi eternidad no tiene medida
como no tienen medida el abismo ni la
  muerte

TWELVE

I don't want anyone else to name me
no one can call me Kopajktzoka
or Helen or Clytemnestra
or Lesbia or Pyokpatzyuwe
no one can say whether they like my hips
or the size of my breasts
Because my soul is immortal
just like the ceiba tree and the volcanoes
just like solitude and silence
and my eternity is boundless
just like death just like the abyss

TUMJAMA MAKA MUJSI'

Tumjama maka' mujsi
jujtzyi'e te' kojama äkpa
nhtä' jame mitkuy'omo
jama'is syi'änhkäjse
nhtyi'ajtyi'opa te' sa'kuy'ora
uj' nhkä'mejtzu
        uj' nhtzam'wiyunhse'aju
Te' nhkojama'is ja' nyiä' irä' näyi'
tzotz'kuy teserike   wyiru'kuy

Y SABRÁS UN DÍA

Y sabrás un día
que el alma duerme
entre calderos de la memoria
como haz de luz
empecinado en quemar amaneceres
No preguntes
          no afirmes
El alma no tiene nombre
ni referencia   ni retorno

AND ONE DAY YOU WILL KNOW

And one day you will know
that the soul sleeps
between memory's cauldrons
like a beam of light
determined to burn up dawns
Don't ask
          don't assert
The soul has no name
no connection   no return

Tä'äjk

ijsyi'ajpajna' sänhkä' pitzä'omoram
watpajna' kayajupä'koroyaram
äj' wejkäis'te myajkpäupä te' kakuy
äjne'rena' te' wane poyo'ajupä sänmänäuk

Metzpatzi' te' yäjkpä tzajy jamemitkuy'isnyi'e
       te' sak'konukskuy ni'is ji' myanepä'
¿Jujtzyi'e nhtä' yajpa yä' janatzapkuy?
¿Jujtzyi'e nhtä' jampäyajpa nhtä' 'toyaram?
Jä'ä
äj' wejkäjinh majkpäutzi te' kakuy
tese' ijtkeruma' kaku'y jomikoroya

Ayer	**Yesterday**
veía luces en oscurana	I saw lights in the darkness
entonaba rapsodias a olvidados	chanted rhapsodies to the forgotten
Fui el grito que desdeñó la muerte	I was the shout that spurned death
el canto que se volvió polvo antes del alba	the song that turned to dust before dawn
Busco el hilo negro del recuerdo	I search for memory's dreadful black thread
el remiendo a esta ausencia	something to mend this loss
¿Cómo deshacer este silencio?	How can I unravel this silence?
¿Cómo contar las horas sin tropezar con la flama?	How can I mark time without stumbling into lava?
Sí	Yes
fui el grito que desdeñó la muerte	I was the shout that spurned death
y tengo aún algo de mortaja en mi mañana	yet her shroud still veils my tomorrow

Nhpet'patzi wane' meya'koroya

tese' te' pänijs'tam wyajna'yajpa
  nhkyomi'ram jokojinh' tujkyajupä
Tyiänh'äyajpa unhtzame pät'koroyaram
  wäkä jana' nhkyäpa'tyi'aä te' sänhkä'
Tyïänh'äyajpa wiyunh'tzame yomo'koroyaram
  wäkä mujsä' myajkpä'yaä te' kämunh

Nhpet'patzi wane te' meya'koroya
yajk' sapäjk'patzi uj nhkopajk jomepä' äj' ijtkuy'omo
äjtzyiä' pitzä'is nhtyi'ona'
äjtzyiä' te' wane jyampä'upä' jama'is

Tejo canciones a la mar
y los hombres entonan rondas
   a sus dioses de estoraque
lanzan diatribas contra ermitaños
   perseguidores de luz
lanzan verdades-oropel a mujeres
   cazadoras de sombras

Tejo canciones a la mar
reposo mis sienes en improvisada
   genealogía
soy el despojo de esta oscuridad
soy la música vedada por la rutina

I weave songs to the sea
and young men chant rounds
   to their resinous gods
they hurl tirades at hermits
   pursuers of light
they hurl bauble-truths at women
   shadow chasers

I weave songs to the sea
I rest my cheek on a makeshift genealogy
I am this darkness' plunder
I am the music that routine denies

Tumjama maka mujsi'
jujtzyie' ijtu toya' temäjk nhtä' sijs'omoram
¡Aj!
Maka' ijsi' jujtzyie' te' kirawa'ane mesyi'a'omopä'
jinhte' mij' mesyi'a'koroya
Mijne'rire' te' kana, te' mayaki'uy
mijnerire' te' jana'tzapkuy teserike te' topya'amyajpapä
mij' mama'is 'wyränhktam
¡Shhhhhhhhhh!

Y sabrás un día
que hay dolores más allá de la piel
¡Ay!
Conocerás que el pan de la mesa
no es el pan de tu mesa
Sólo es tuya la sal y la amargura
sólo tuyo el silencio y los ojos
lacerantes de tu Madre
¡Shhhhhhhhhhh!

And one day you will know
there is pain deeper than flesh
Ay!
You will understand that the bread on the
	table
is not bread for your table
For you only bitterness and salt
only the silence and knives
in the eyes of Mother Earth
Shhhhhhhhhhh!

Jäyä känhkuy'syi'e myetzyi'ajpapä wenis'tam
wäkä jäyäjse jyamyaä 'wynh'tam
maka jutmini' te' kipsoki'uy
maka nyiäpuri' yoma'
toyas' tzyi'uräk'omopä
maka' kyake' te' peka'ijtyi'ajupä
jomepä pänh'omoram, pänayajpapä
anhuku'is 'kyämunh'omoram

Maka äwi' te' meya'
kyäwo'ropapä'is te' nasakopajk
'kyäwäro'japyapa'is mij' 'kojama
maka poks'pake pyatu'kam
wane' jana'tzame'omopä

Como polen que abejas cazan
para sentirse flores
esparcirá la conciencia
departirá sus aromas
en cada comisura del dolor
sustituirá el vacío de las tardes
por los nuevos hombres que nacen
bajo sombras de los ancestros

Se calmará el mar
el que rodea la tierra
y el que rodea tu alma
se calmará cuando halle
música dentro del silencio

Like the pollen bees seek
to feel as flowers do
consciousness will scatter
sharing its aromas
in every wailing mouth of pain
the afternoon's emptiness will be filled
by new relations born
in the ancestors' shadows

The sea encircling
the earth will settle
and encircling your soul
will settle when music
is found in silence.

Tujkpa makapä’ tuki’ ne’ nhtä’ jo’koyuk
                ne’ nhtä’ maya’uk
täjkäpya nhtä’ mapasyi’omo
tum’wirupa nhtä’ ijtkuj’yinh
Komejkoyajpa te’ pänh’tam
kyomejkyajpa jaye’ijstam
                        toto jaye’istam
                                tzapkuy’istam

Tese…
te’ ijtkuy teserike te’ kakuy nhte’jurore’ makapä tujkya’e
makapäre’ mytya’e ji’ nhtä’ nijamepä jama’omo

La caída de fruto llega en cada esperanza
        en cada pesimismo
ella penetra sueños
se convulsiona con el destino
La gente miente
mienten los libros
        los periódicos
          las noticias

Más...
el tiempo y la muerte son cántaros de agua
saliendo de la boca del día

Fruit rots alongside every hope
        alongside every despair
she pierces dreams
mingles with destiny
Everyone lies
books
        newspapers
          the news

And yet...
time and death are vases of water
the day exhales

TE' KOJAMA WI'RUPA JURÄ NITIYÄ JI' NHTÄ MANEMÄ'

Nyi'ojsujse
nyi'apujse
uka' käräjku ore'
uka' käräjku ansänh
maka mij jasinsate
punsate
mij' 'kojama

—ORE'OMOPÄ KONUKSKUY

Te' kojama wi'rupa jurä nitiyä ji' nhtä manemä'
wirupa wäkä 'yukä' meya'nä
nä' nhtyajupä'jinh
wynapä kyänhtätzä
nä' jurä Nasakopajk'is kyojt'päu myusokyuy
nä'kanapa'ajkpä jurü' nhtä' nhkomi'is tzyajku
syijsis'yoma'

Te' kojama'is nyiäputpa natz'kuy
nyiäpujt'pa kajsoj'kuy
myetzpa poyo'is syiänhkä'
myetzpa winapä ijtku'yijs jy'uwi'
Tese' te' wiränhk'nä mutpa tuj'omoram
mutpa winhtutzi'omo
jurü nhtä' amyajpa
kayajupä

64   Mikeas Sánchez

EL ALMA RETORNA AL GRITO DEL SILENCIO

¿Fue por tus faenas?
¿Por tus grandes penas?
¿Ofendiste con tu discurso?
¿Deshonraste a la Luz por impulso?
Voy a sanarte,
renovarte
el alma

—ORACIÓN ZOQUE

El alma retorna al grito del silencio
  retorna a beber agua de mar
    con que sació su
      primera sed
agua de vida donde la tierra depositó sus
  arcanos
agua de salitre dulcísima donde Dios dejó
  esencias de su cuerpo

El alma desecha misticismos
  desecha esperanzas
busca reflejos de arena
busca brasas de soledad
Y su ojo de agua brota en gotas de lluvia
  en el rabillo del ojo
    para mirar fantasmas

THE SOUL RETURNS TO SILENCE'S CRY

Was it for your actions?
For your suffering?
Did your words offend?
Did your urges dishonor Providence?
I will heal you,
renew
your soul

—ZOQUE PRAYER

The soul returns to silence's cry
  returns to drink the seawater that
    first slaked its thirst
      life-giving
water where the earth hid its mysteries
sweetest saltpeter where traces of God's
  body linger

The soul casts aside mysticisms
  and hopes
seeks the sand's glimmer
seeks solitude's embers
And from the corner an eye
  where we glimpse ghosts
    its spring wells up in
      raindrops

Ji' nhwiyunhse'aje jama'is kyajkse
ji' nhwiyunhse'aje wenenh'omo te' sijkutyam
te' joko'kyutyam
Tese' nhtä' ijtkutyam kätupä jinam' nhwyru'i
te'omo maka te' kakuy'is tzyame
te'omo tumä mama'is jyampäpa'yune
Jiksekanhte nyitzäjk'papä te' popyapä ijtkuy
jiksekanhte nhtä' makapä jurä'
nhtä' supa'

Las grietas del tiempo se equivocan
también se equivocan sonrisas
                        esperas
Y la vida no se retracta
sus manos acompasan adagios de muerte
        acompasan la separación madre-hijo
entonces el éxodo inicia
                        se libera

Time's cracks make mistakes
smiles and hopes
                        make mistakes too
And life does not recant
its hands keep time with deathly refrains
        keep time with mother-child
                        separation
so the exodus begins
                        she's freed

Te' kojama'is nyiäpujtpa omoma'ram
nyiäpujtpa musokyuy wänyi'ajupä
'yajk tzojkapyatzi äj' nhtoya'
myetzpa wäpä ijtkuy
    yayipä mapasyi'omoram
jyapya kasäjkuy-kiskuy
    wäkä' nhtä jamkapä'ä nhtä' yakpajk'kajkuy

Äj nhkojama jäyäre'
jäyänä're' ne myetzupä'is nä'
    koko'nä' pekapä
pekajse te' toya'

El alma emana perfumes
exhala secretos de la especie
reconforta lo apartado de mis penas
busca óbolos de paz
   en colinas del sueño
traza esferas de astucia-ternura
   para compensar soledades

Mi alma
orquídea de amatista buscando agua
   agua de coco antiguo
tan antiguo como el dolor

The soul exudes fragrances
exhales secrets of the species
comforts my most hidden shames
searches for obols of peace
   in hills of dream
traces circles of tender cunning
   to counterbalance solitudes

My soul
amethyst orchid seeking water
   ancient coconut water
as ancient as pain

Te' anima'is 'jyame ponyi yajpa
ponyi' yajpajse te' topyapä' ijtku'y
ponyi' kisyi'kapajse te' kaku'y
Tä'äjk mapasyi'nhkomi'is
'wyajnayajpana' 'nhka'eram toya isyi'ajupä
ja' jyajmaya'äpäis myayi'is nyi'ujtzkä

Yäti te' mapasyi'komi wijtpa
tokoyupäjse, tyi'okoyu 'kyasäjkuy
¿Juräpä tzajpijs 'yona'omo tzäyu'
wäpä' mapasyi?
¿Juräpä' sa'ä'omo te' tzu' jonhtzyi'is
nyi'umu' te' anhsänhk?

La memoria del alma tiene una extinción
  lenta
tan lenta como la primera soledad
tan arisca como la muerte
Ayer el ángel del sueño
levitaba canciones a niños desérticos
esparcía besos a aquellos que no
  conmutaron calores maternos

Ahora el ángel deambula
perdió sus ojos imantados de azul
¿En qué lugar del cielo quedó guarecida
la inocencia del sueño?
¿En qué despertar el ave nocturna
se robó las horas?

The soul's memory slowly goes extinct
as slowly as the loneliness of being born
as irascibly as death
Yesterday the angel of sleep
raised songs to deserted children
sprinkled kisses on those missing maternal
  warmth

Now the angel wanders
he lost his magnetic blue eyes
Where in heaven did the innocence of
  dreams
find safe haven?
On which waking did the night bird
steal the dreamtime journey?

Yä mojksepä' najsis'tzyi'okoyis nhtyajk kasäjpa
tyajk jampäpa' mäjapä mayakyuy
yajk popa' jäyäram tzajpomo
Wirupatzi äj' motzyi'une ijtkuy'omo
putzyiä'rampä' jama'omo
      täjkäkämä'rampä'
        poyewyjt'kuy'omoram

Wirupatzi äj' motzyi'une ijtkuy'omo
nhtzäjk'wyrupatzi more'kutkuy
mäjtzä'nhwyru'patzi "käwänhkuy'mätzik" tzayi'koroya
wäkä' nhtzäjkna'tzyi'aä' joyjoyeram
¿Juräpä murä'omo
tzäyaju te' peka'tzäkiram?

Esta tierra corazón de maíz entusiasma
hace olvidar tristezas de piedra
hace renacer el cielo tapizado de flores
Vuelvo al encuentro infantil
días amarillos
          callejones jugando al destino

Vuelvo al encuentro infantil
pasteles de lodo
juegos "escondidillas" a la tarde
canciones que se cantan para asustar
    duendes
¿En qué pozo de la suerte
quedaron los recuerdos?

This corn-hearted land thrills me
makes me forget my rock-hard sorrows
revives the sky carpeted with flowers
I return to childhood memories
golden days
          alleyways imagining where fate
          would take us

I return to childhood memories
mudpies
afternoon games of hide-and-seek
songs to scare duendes away
Which of fate's wells
holds my memories?

Ne' sutu' 'wyrä' tanhtanh'jinh
wäkä nhkäwä' te' tzajp
ne' sutu' nhtumä' 'äj jana'tzame
meya'upu'is nhwyaj'yinh
ne' sutu' mparä' meya'is tzyi'okoy
'tyi'okoyajupä suksyi'ajupäis
teserike myetzyi'apapäma a'a'pänistam
nu'a'yomo'is wyane'omo

¿Juwa' makyajpa' te' popo'ranhtanh'tam
'kyäkiaj'papäis te' tzajp?
¿Juwä' nukpa' te' kojama' peyase'wejpapä?

Quiero peregrinar con mariposas
y tapizar el cielo
quiero unir mi silencio
con cabelleras del oleaje
quiero encontrar el corazón del mar
que perdieron los ahogados
y que los navegantes siguen buscando
en cantos de sirenas

¿A dónde emigran las mariposas blancas
que tapizan el cielo?
¿Dónde arriba el alma y su alarido de
    halcón?

I want to join the pilgrimage of butterflies
and cloak the sky
I want to braid my silence
with curling waves
I want to find the depths of the sea
that those who drowned lost
those the seafarers still seek
in the sirens' songs

Where do the white butterflies
that cloak the sky migrate?
Where does the soul's falcon cry alight?

Äj' nhkojama jekä're
yajk' katyopapä'is 'nhwyt
te' najs'tzika tajsupä
oktubre poya'omo
te' nä'tzyika ijtpamä te' anhsänhk
teserike nä' itzyi'ram

Äjtzyi'ä' tza' wyänupäis musoki'uy
tese' metzpatzi äj' nhtzokoy' mosapyä mapasyi'is' myätzik'omo
  metzpatzi te' tokoyupä mapasyi' äj' anhuku'isnyi'eram
    te' yajksyi'u'ijtkuy 'tä karampapä'omo
mitajse'naka sawa'is syijkuy

Es mi alma la agonía postrera
del suicida arrepentido
el cántaro que se llenó de lluvia
en tardes de octubre
el agua de pozo donde mora el tiempo
y sus monstruos marinos

Soy quimera de los secretos de mármol
y busco mi corazón en el quinto juego del
    letargo
        busco ese sueño perdido de mis
        antepasados
                esa soledad de morir la vida
en cada beso del viento

My soul is the final agony
of a repentant suicide
a clay vessel filled with rain
on October afternoons
the wellwater where time
and its sea monsters dwell

I am a chimera of secrets in stone
seeking my heart in deepest sleep
        seeking my ancestors' lost dreaming
            this solitude of a life spent dying
in the wind's every kiss

Äj' nhkojama'is nyiä ijtu' tiram' jinhmusipä' tzyi'amä
pujtpapä' anhäpyak te' tuj'
Te' topyapä ijtkuy sapa' äj' wyränhk aknyi'a'omo
    tese maka' jamopyapä 'äj wiränhk'omo
Kuko'sopya kotzäjkäjsi
kokyp'sopya äj atzypä'jara'is myotzy'anhtunh'omoram
—uj nhkojama'is yätzpäpa sapila teserike topyapä'ajy—
Tese' te' topyapä'ijtkuy' pujtpa kujktzu'omo
    poya wena'omo

Tengo silencios en el alma
crujiendo con la lluvia
Y la soledad amanece de mi ojo
  izquierdo a mi ojo derecho
espía desde ciclos volcánicos
medita desde ventanas de mis abuelos
—vomita sábila y ajenjo—
La soledad se liberta a media noche
  en médula lunar

My soul has silences
rustling with the rain
And loneliness dawns from my left eye
  to my right
keeps watch from volcanic cycles
ponders from my grandparents' windows
—vomits aloe and wormwood—
Loneliness is set free at midnight
  in moon's marrow

Äj jame? yäjkpä' kajare'
   jinam' mapä nhwyru'i
¿Jujtzyi'e nhtzäjkpa wäkä' mujsä nukä ijtumä meya nä'
   nä' kana'pa'ajkpä
¿Jujtzyi'e nhyajpa yä' tokoki'uy?
äj' nhkäram takyajpa 'pikpak'käjsi te' nä'
jinakste' äjtzi' te' toya
te' yajkpä wiränhk tzyajk'papä ne' yajk" ka'upäis nhwyt
Metspatzi' äj' jara, metzapyatzi pu'apä' nhkyasäj'kuy

Mi memoria es caja negra
  de un avión sin regreso
¿Cómo llego a la libación del agua de mar
  del agua de salitre dulcísimo?
¿Cómo justifico este extravío?
Mis manos se quiebran con el contacto del
  agua
quién soy sino el contrapunto del dolor
la perla negra en ojos del suicida
Y busco a mi padre y su macilenta alegría

My memory is a lost plane's
  black box
How do I reach the libation of seawater
  of such sweet saltpeter?
How do I justify this inebriation of loss?
My hands shatter at contact with water
who am I if not pain's counterpoint
the black pearl in a suicide's eyes
And I search for my father and his pallid
  joy

Te' ijtumäna winapä' äj' nhtäjk
manhpatzi ne' yanh'äyupä nä"
tese jinhte' meya'is ne' onoyupä'
tuj'te' ne nhkyejku täjkäjsi'
Myinhtyi'otzum te' "tuj'poya"
nhtä' mujstampam maka'mujya'e nhtä nhkoso'ram

Ä'kpamätzi yäti' jinam' kyeke tuj'
Ji kyeke' tzu'nä'
ji kyeke' jap'
          ji kyeke' poyo'
anh'ä'kyä'rire' nhtä" manhpa
ijtyaju jaye, sänhkä' ma'a'ijs'nyi'e
ä'kpamätzi yäti"
ja' iräm äj' atzyipä'jara
aku'ajkupä nhwyiränh'jinh
metza'ora' naptzu'isnyi'e'omo

Desde la casa en que no estoy
escucho el danzar de las olas
y no es el mar quien me habla
es la lluvia que azota el tejado
Ha llegado "el norte"
y todos sabemos que se mojaran los pies

Donde duermo ya no llueve
Ni gotas de agua
ni sílice
     ni arena
sólo ruidos de autos
letreros y luces neón
Donde duermo
ya no está mi abuelo
con sus ojos desnudos
a las dos de la mañana

From the house I've left behind
I hear the waves' dancing
and it's not the sea that speaks to me
it's the rain whipping the tin roof
The north wind has arrived
and we all know our feet will get wet

Where I sleep it no longer rains
Not drops of water
not limestone
     not sand
only cars' noises
signs and neon lights
Where I sleep
my grandfather no longer
opens his naked eyes
at two in the morning

AISHA'

Kyiä'wänhpa tyi'ojtzkämä'
te' takapyä'yoma' nhtyi'omo'ajkuy'isnyi'e
te' Espanyi'a te' Marru'ekos
tere' tumü' papinyi'omo juka'putzäpä'
tijanh tzyi'anhkapä'
wiyunh ampapä'
tzyi'ajku' Marrakesyi'
nhtä' 'pojyaj'pyajse nhtä' nhkämunk
nhtä' nhtenhpä'japyajse sänhkä', tajsupä'poyaram
Hachis'omoma, tzoyu'yoki'uy tojksupä'
nhtä' sukpa' tyi'äjkmä', nhtä' sukpa nyi'aka'omo

Myama'is tzyi'ajmayu
jana' tyena' tome' kätnäm'pamä'
            jana' tyena' tome'
            motzyi'anhtunh'mä'
                    jana' tyena' tome' sutkuy'mä'
myama'is kyutzyi'u
te'. takapyä yomoma' tyojtz'jisnyi'e
te' jawaki'uy tzyi'ejkisnyi'e
yomo' ne' jyokupäis winapä' jyaya'

Hachís'omoma kanela'omoma
maka' yajk' soje' yasa'käjsi
wäkä' te' jyaya'is jana' kyomujsa'
eyarampä' pänis'yomoma wyänupä nyi'aka'is
Hachís'omoma, yerpapu'ena'omoma
maka' nhtzyi'i myama'

AISHA

Guarda debajo de su lengua
la sensación amarga de su sexo
en España como en Marruecos
sigue siendo la muchacha cobriza
de anchas caderas
y ojos exactos
Dejó Marrakech
como quien huyendo de su propia sombra
evita los faroles y la luna llena
Olor a hachís y té verde
se siente en su casa y en su piel

Su madre le advirtió de los peligros
de acercarse demasiado a los puentes
                y a los balcones
                        y a los amores
su madre le compartió
la sensación amarga en la lengua
el ardor en su vientre
de mujer guardándose para su primer amor

Olor a hachís y canela
le untará a su vestido de boda
para que el esposo no revele
el olor que su piel guarda de otros hombres
Olor a hachís y hierbabuena
le ofrecerá a su madre
para que su vientre albergue un hijo

AISHA

Guards the bitter taste of her sex
beneath her tongue
in Spain as in Morocco
remains the coppery girl
with wide hips
and sharp eyes
She left Marrakesh
like someone fleeing their own shadow
avoiding streetlamps and the full moon
the scent of green tea and hashish
emanates from her home and skin

Her mother warned her of the dangers
of getting too close to bridges
                and balconies
                        and lovers
her mother shared with her
the bitter taste on her tongue
the burning in her womb
of a woman saving herself for her first love

She will anoint her wedding dress
with the scent of hashish and cinnamon
so that her groom does not discover
the scent of other men that lingers on her
   skin
She will offer her mother
the scent of hashish and mint

wäkä' nhtzyi'ejkomo nhtyi'enh'a tumä une'
hachís'omoma kanela'omoma
wäkä' nhkyomi' Ala'is nhtzyiä tumü nhka'e
wäkä 'nhkyomi' Ala'is myasanh'äjya jyaya'is tyiämpu

olor a hachís y canela
para que Alah le dé un niño
para que Alah bendiga la semilla de su
   varón

so that her womb might hold a son
the scent of hashish and cinnamon
so that Allah will give her a son
so that Allah will bless her man's seed

RAMA

Te' sutkuy tumä' pajkte' jairäpä' is nyi' äyi.'
—JULIETA VALERO

Jojpajkinh tajsu' syis'
tajsu nhtyi'om'ijtkuy, yune'ijtkuy
nyiä' ijtu' ips'komajk'ko'mojsay ame'
teje' myusapya Mahomas nhkyis'kuy
uka' nyiä' ijtpa patzoke'une
tekoroya jyokpa jyaya
jäyä'tzäkipä' ya'sakämä
sutkuy kämä'
ponyipä konuks'kuyjinh
konukspä tzu'ko'tzu'
wäkä myajkpä'ä sutkuyis' nhtyi'oya
Kasujpa tä' äkpa' jana'pama
uka' ni'ijs ji' nhtä' pike' nhtä yom'ijtkuy
teje' nhkipspa' sone'naka
yanka'myajpasenh'omo wyrunh'tam
tese' myapa'syi'äpya' Dakar'pä kupkuy
juwä sone' yäjk'tampä yomo'istam
ne' pyäjkinh'tzyi'oki'aju pyapy'nyi'omo'ajkutyi'am
tumtumäpä'is wyatpa peka'wane wolof'ore'omo
tumtumäpä papynyi'omo nä' jonhtzyi're'
ne' syirijtupä sutkuy'käjsi

RAMA

El deseo es un hueso al que nadie puso nombre.

—JULIETA VALERO

Los ríos que la habitan
se bifurcan entre su infancia y su sexo
tiene treinta y cinco años
y sabe que Mahoma no le perdonará
un hijo sin padre
por eso su vientre espera con calma
debajo de su vestido de flores
debajo de la pasión
desde una plegaria silenciosa
que pronuncia cada noche
para ahuyentar los malestares de la carne
Ser libre es dormir desnuda
sin unas manos buscando tu sexo
piensa mil veces
mientras cierra los ojos
y se sueña en una calle de Dakar
entre una decena de muchachas negras
recién llegadas a la pubertad
cada una ensaya cánticos ancestrales en
    wólof
cada una es una gaviota salvaje
volando alrededor del deseo

RAMA

Desire is a bone that no one named.

—JULIETA VALERO

The rivers that course through her
split between childhood and pubescence
she is thirty-five years old
and knows that Mohammed will not
    forgive her
a fatherless son
so her womb calmly waits
beneath her flowered dress
beneath passion
from a quiet prayer
that she utters each night
to drive away the discomfort of the flesh
To be free is to sleep naked
with no hands seeking your sex
she thinks a thousand times
as she closes her eyes
and dreams she's on a street in Dakar
with a dozen young Black women
newly arrived at puberty
each one rehearsing ancestral canticles in
    Wolof
each one is a wild gull
circling desire

MUMURE' NHTÄ' YÄJKTAMPÄ

'Tä' komi' uka' yijtupäre
tejurä' mij' jamtzäjkpatzi'
—NANCY MOREJÓN

Ni'is ji' myusaya'e nyiäyiram
teserike kyonuksku'tyam aku'ajkyajpapä'jinh te' anhtunh'tam
tzajpis'nyi'e teserike yatzipä'räjk'kisnyi'e
Wijtyi'ajpapä'koroya yäjktampä' pänh'tamte'
jomemi'tyajupäma Barcelona'kupkuy'omo
jana' yosyi'kuyjinh'tampä
ji' myusyi'a'e'päis tzyi'apya'ä kastiya'ore
yäjktampä pänhtam' makyapapä tunh'omo
ma'a' wyjtyi'ajpapä
pänh'tam yisanh'sajyaj'papä'is yose' teserike nyi'atzku'tyam
eyapäis wynanh'omoram
Te'is nyiä' ijtyaju nhkyomi
äjtzi ijtkeruri äj' nhkomi
tese' yajk' maya'yajpatzi tyi'oyaistam
myajk'kyaräjpa'ankä te mossos d'esquadras'tam
jujtzyi'e myta' yanhku'kamä'yaräi
yajk' tumya'räi numyajpapä'jinh teserike yajka'oye'jinh'tam
Wenenh'omo makatzi mujapä tunh'omo
makatzi Barceloneta makatzi Ramblas
tese' a'myajpatzi mumu' te' yäjtampä pänhtam
tyi'okyajpapäis popo'pä tyi'uku' najs'käjsi
makajse wyruya'e mäja' meya'omo
makajse nu'kya'e syi'utya'räjpamä
te' kupkuy' jina' yispäjkya'epä, nhkysa'yaräjpamä'

TODOS SOMOS CIMARRONES

Oh dios si existes
No he dudado de tu existencia
    —NANCY MOREJÓN

Nadie conoce sus nombres
ni sus ruegos que abrirían todas las
   aduanas
del cielo y del infierno
Para los viandantes sólo son negros
recién llegados a Barcelona
sin empleo
sin español en la lengua
cimarrones que van por la calle
con su venta improvisada de baratijas
gente que extiende su hambre y su
   asombro
ante la mirada de turistas y fisgones
Ellos tienen un Dios
yo tengo un Dios
y me lamento por su mala suerte
de correr cada vez que los mossos
   d'esquadra
vienen tras de ellos a encarcelarlos
a juntarlos con ladrones y homicidas
A veces voy por la Gran Avenida
o por la Barceloneta o por las Ramblas
y veo a todos aquellos hombres negros
que extienden su manta blanca sobre el piso

WE'RE ALL MAROONS

Oh god if you exist
I've never doubted your existence
    —NANCY MOREJÓN

No one knows their names
or their pleas that would open every border
in heaven and hell
To the passerby they're just Black men
newly arrived in Barcelona
no job
no Spanish on their tongues
Maroons who walk the street
hawking trinkets
their hunger and angst put on display
before the gaze of nosy tourists
They have a God
I have a God
and I rue their bad luck
having to run every time the Mossos
   d'Esquadra
chase them to jail
lumping them in with thieves and
   murderers
Sometimes I go down La Gran Avenida
or down the Barceloneta or down Las
   Ramblas
and I see all those Black men
spreading their white blankets on the ground

Jiksekanhte' tzäpyapä tekoroya'ram
topyapä'tzokoy
te' tyi'umpä konuks'kuy
juwä' mujspa' jonh'tzyijse' toyapäjk'kya'ä
Te'is nyiä' ijtyaju tumä nhkyomi tanä'ompapä
kyäwä'nyi'ajpapä kyämunh'nhkämä
une'is wyanh'janhmoky'usyi'e
yajka'oye'is wyanh'janhmoky'usyi'e
Tekoroya tuj'omo
mumu' kasäjpa watyajpa
jyampä'yajpa yä' mäja'kupkuy
jurä ni'is ji' nhjyajm'jayaräi nyi'oyiram
Te'istam nyiä' ijtyi'aju nhkyomiram
sunyi' ompapä
nyiä' ijtyajkeruri' tumä popo'ruku
aku'ajkpapä sunyi anhkam'papä
nyiä' ijtyaju tumä ma'a
wäkä jana' yos'kaya'ä
nyiä' ijtyaju tumä popo'ruku nhtä' pakspapä nhtä' sinh'papä
wäkä mujsä pyoya'ä ya'yi
jene yayi ji' nhkyäpatyi'a'emä te' mossos d'esquadras'tam
ji' nhkyäpatyi'a'emä te' nhkysa'yajpapäis yäjktampä pänhtam
ji' nhkyäpatyi'a'emä nhtä' nhkomi'is tyi'o'tyi'ajkuyis

como si de pronto volvieran al mar
y ondearan las velas de la tierra prometida
la tierra que un día se les volvió espejismo
Entonces sólo les queda la barca
de sus corazones a la deriva
la piedra del naufragio
donde cada uno es un pájaro que gime
Pero ellos tienen un Dios
que guardan bajo su sombra
con la fe de un niño
y la esperanza de un suicida
Por eso aún bajo la lluvia
todos cantan su mala suerte
y a ninguno le importa esta ciudad
que no sabe pronunciar sus nombres
Porque ellos tienen un Dios que huele a
    acacias
que sabe a éter y soledad
Y también tienen una manta blanca
que se abre y cierra fácilmente
una venta improvisada de baratijas
para sostener el hambre
una manta que se dobla y amarra
para poder correr lejos
muy lejos de los mossos d'esquadra
de la xenofobia
y de la ceguera de Dios

as if they'll soon return to sea
flying the sail of the promised land
the land that became a mirage
So all they have left is the drifting
dinghy of their hearts
the castaway's jagged rocks
where each is a distressed bird
But they have a God
that they hold close
with the faith of a child
and the hope of a suicide
That's why even in the rain
they all sing their bad luck
and none of them care about this city
that can't pronounce their names
Because they have a God that smells of
    acacia
that tastes of ether and loneliness
And they each have a white blanket
that easily opens and closes
hawking trinkets
to sustain the hungry
a sheet that can be folded and tied up
so they can run far
far away from the Mossos d'Esquadra
from xenophobia
from God's blindness

NEREYDA'IS MYAPASYI'ÄYU NHWYT NEW'YORK

Nereyda'is myapasyiäyu nhwyt New'York
ne' yamumä' kyene tumä tuku' ma'a'omo nyiäyipäis Macy's
tumä ore'yomo
tumä papinyi'omo pänajupä' nhtä' najs'omoram
tumä' nhkya'e ne' pyoyupä kosyi'taksi'
ne' nhtzyajk'kyenpä'upäis nhtyakpajk'ajku'y
'Yanh'uku'is myuja'ajkuj'syi'e
jaya' iri' nijuräpä kupkuy nasakopajk'omo
yäjse' tejse' yenh'u' ojse'jinh
te' nhkyä'ram takyajupä paka'kijs
kawa' wä' yispäjkyaju te' tzama ja' yispäjkia'äjse syis'
jiksek' nhkyomi te' nasakopajk'
Tzitzunh'kätzäjk'mäpä
tumä mätzik' wane'rire'na
juwä' 'yakpajk'unestam' wyä'nyi'ayajpana nyi'atzkutyam
Tese te Pinakate jenere'na natz'kusyi'epä'
tumä ne' 'mpyakä'yupä' papinyi'omo'koroya
tese' te' täjtzupä'najs Sonorasnyi'e' jenere'na mujapä'
wäkä pya'taya'ä' 'mpyajk' käwanupä poyo'omoram
Nereyda'is myapasyi'äyu nhwyt New'York
ne' yamumä' nhkyene tumä tuku'ma'a'omo nyiäyi'päis Macy's
Nasakopajk' uka' mujspa manä'
minä' pinhja' 'yanima
minä' yajk' tzunhja' kyänh'tätzä' tumä'moneko'
/majkis 'yames'nyi'e
minä' näpujta' nhtyajk'syi'u'tzäjk'kayajupä' syis'
minä' yajk' tujk'wyruä kya'e'omo
te' nhkya'e myäjtzä'pyapäsna tza'uneram

NEREYDA SE SOÑÓ EN NEW YORK

Nereyda se soñó en New York
contemplando su reflejo en un escaparate
   de Macy's
una ore'yomo migrante
una muchacha nacida en imperio Tzitzunh
una niña huyendo descalza
lo más lejos posible de la orfandad
Jamás la grandeza de su linaje
habrá de compararse con la de ningún otro
   reino
pero creció con hambre
y sus manos agrietadas por el frío
conocieron mejor el campo que su propio
   cuerpo
entonces Nasakopajk' desde la
   majestuosidad del Tzitzunh'kätzäjk'
era sólo una cajita de música
donde las huérfanas guardaban su espanto
Pero el Pinacate era demasiado agreste
para una muchacha con frío
pero el desierto de Sonora era muy grande
para hallar su esqueleto encorvado entre
  las dunas
Nereyda se soñó en New York
contemplando su reflejo en un escaparate
   de Macy's
Oh Nasakopajk' si puedes escucharla

NEREYDA DREAMED IN NEW YORK

Nereyda dreamed in New York
contemplating her reflection in a Macy's
   window
a migrant Ore'yomo
a girl born in the Tzitzunh empire
a girl fleeing barefoot
as far from orphanhood as possible
The grandness of her lineage could never
be compared to any other kingdom
but she grew up hungry
and her hands chapped by the cold
knew the countryside better than her own
   body
so Nasakopajk' from the majesty
   of the Tzitzunh'kätzäjk'
was just a music box
where the orphan girls kept their fear
But the Pinacate was too rugged
for a trembling girl
but the Sonora desert was too large
to find her skeleton hunched among the
   dunes
Nereyda dreamed in New York
contemplating her reflection in a Macy's
   window
Oh Nasakopajk' if you can hear her
draw near to gather her soul

ijtyajupä te' tzitzunh'kotzäjkis'myi'eya'omo
minä' tejinh' käminä'
minä'

acércate a recoger su alma

acércate a saciar su sed de 500 años

acércate a rescatar su cuerpo injuriado

acércate a convertirla de nuevo en niña

aquella que jugaba con los guijarros

que circundan el cráter del Tzitzunh

acércate a ella

acércate

draw near to satiate her 500-year thirst

draw near to rescue her injured body

draw near to turn her back into that girl

who played with the pebbles

from around Tzitzunh's crater

draw near to her

draw near

Jujtzyere sone' ka'nä'upä 'tä' ujtzyi'omoram.
Jujtzyi'e kaku'y 'tä' nä' ijta'u 'tä' nekäomoram.

—VICENTE HUIDOBRO

¡Jä! te' kakuy myojna'pyapä'is mij' nhkojso
yakpajk unej'se
yajk' tzuts'papä'is pa'ajk'pa'ajk
jyo'kopyasenh'omo
¿Tiya' jok'pa?

Cuántas cosas han muerto adentro de nosotros.

Cuánta muerte llevamos en nosotros.

—VICENTE HUIDOBRO

¡Ay! de la muerte que te cubre los pies
como a un niño desamparado
que te amamanta dulcemente
mientras esperas
¿Qué esperas?

So many things have died inside of us.

How much death we carry within.

—VICENTE HUIDOBRO

Ay! From the death that covers your feet
like a helpless child
that sweetly suckles
while you wait
What are you waiting for?

Maka' mini' te' kakuy

tese' maka 'mpyi'are' mij' änhkuy'omo
maka 'mpyi'are' mij' nhtäjkijs myuka'omoram
jiksekanhte te' yäjkpä tanhtanh'is
maka'pä tzyajme jujtzyi'ekte makapä nhkya'e
Jiksekanhte' makapä jampä'i mij' näyi'
maka nhtyuki' tumä mapasyi'
te' mapasyi' ja' tyujkäpä tzayi'kam
u te' mapasyi' yakpajk'unesnyi'e
tese' nyi'akpajk'unemareke' mijtzi

Llegará la muerte

y te encontrará en tu cama

entre los hongos que habitan tu casa

o en el recuerdo de la mariposa negra

que anticipó tu ausencia

Entonces olvidarás tu nombre

y te volverás un sueño

el sueño de una tarde jamás contemplada

o el sueño del niño desamparado que fuiste

y no has dejado de ser

Death will arrive

and find you in your bed

surrounded by the mushrooms invading
   your home

or in the memory of the black moth

that foretold your absence

Then you will forget your name

and become a dream again

the dream of an afternoon never before
   imagined

or the dream of the helpless child that you
   were

and have not stopped being

Maka mini te' kaku'y

te' wiyunh'sepä
     te' nhtä' totzyi'äjk'papä'is
maka' nhwyajte' mij' nhkä'
maka' 'nhtyi'äkmäni' mäja'pitzä'omo
jiksekanhte makapä nhkomujsi'
jujtzyi'e ijtyi'aju jäkya'jupä tzaräjk
tem'nhtyi'emä wänhpamä mij' nhtoya

Llegará la muerte
la verdadera
        la tirana
atará tus manos
te aventará al abismo
y sólo entonces sabrás
que hay vacíos más profundos
que la soledad que guardas

Death will arrive
the true one
            the tyrant
it will bind your hands
it will hurl you into the abyss
and only then will you know
there is a deeper emptiness
than the solitude you keep

Wäkä nhtä' jampä'ä te' toya'

wä' nhtä' konuksä'
wäkä' tä' jampä'oya
wä' nhtä' jampä'ä te' toya
nhtä' pajk'omopä
Yajk' ya'ä' te' kakuyis'
           nhjyame
Pijstinh'omo yajk' tujk'wyruä
          äj' nhkojama
Wäkä' nhtä' jampä'ä te' toya'
Wäk'tire' nhtä' jambä'ä nhtä' näyi'

Que para olvidar el dolor
sólo baste una plegaria
que para el olvido
el dolor se compacte
más adentro de mis huesos
Que se borre la memoria
                de mi muerte
que en ceiba se convierta
              mi alma
que para olvidar el dolor
baste con olvidar mi nombre

May just one prayer
be enough to forget your pain
May my aches compact
deep in my bones
May the memory of my death
              be erased
may my soul become
              a ceiba
may simply forgetting my name
be enough to forget your pain

Äkyaj'papä temäjk kätpamä te' jama teserike te' tzu'
te' ijtyajupä temäjk toya'omo, mayakyuy'omo
mapasyiäyajpa te' ijtkuy'jinh
nyi'atzyajpa te' ijtkuy
¿Isaj' ji' nyi'atze'?
Tese' jinhma̱' ne' nhtä' kara'upäis
nhtä' jam'nhtzäjktampa te' ka'yajupä
tä' sijktampa nhtä' nhtoya''omoram
tä' ka'rampa jama'ko'jama
Tese' nhtyajk' tastampa'is nhtä' maya'kyutyam
eyapä'is kyaj'säjkyuy'jinhtam
mayayaj'ketapäri
nhtä' mapasyiä'tyampa te' ijtku'y
Nhtä' metztampa eyapä' ijtkuy
nhtä' nhtzajk'tyi'orampa te' natz'kuy

**Los que duermen más allá del día y la
noche**

más allá de la soledad y del abandono
sueñan con la vida
y les asusta vivir
¿A quién no le asusta?
Y los que estamos despiertos
los que vivimos ausencias
desde la soledad de las sonrisas
quienes morimos a cada instante
y nos consolamos llenando vacíos
con la alegría de cuerpos
igualmente vacíos
También soñamos con vivir
habitar siluetas
escapar del espanto

Those who sleep beyond day and night

beyond solitude and abandonment
dream of life
and are scared to live
Who isn't scared to?
And we who are awake
we who survive absence
with lonely smiles
we who die each instant
and console ourselves by filling emptiness
with the joy of bodies
equally empty
We also dream of living
inhabiting shadows
escaping terror

Mujspatzi nyitzäjk'pak teserike yajpak' te' jama

nitisepä tiyä' jinh' ma' nhtyi'okoye

nhkokips'kuy

teserike' äj' näyis'nyi'äpinh'oma

Mumu ti'is wyunhpa nhkyene

te' tzayi'is wyunhpa nhwyane

te' tzä'is wyunhpa pytzä'ajkuy

Tese'

jojmo' äj' nhtzokoyis myuspa

tumä maya'kyuy

yajk' tasa'pyapä'is äj' nhkojama

te' ka'kuy nhte' jurore

makapä tuki'

En el inicio y la culminación del día sé
que no ha de perderse nada
ni el pensamiento
ni el olor a sangre de mi nombre
Todo conserva sus formas
la tarde y su sonata
la noche y su temblor de piernas
Sin embargo
lejos del augurio
una perturbación
inunda el pozo de mi alma
la muerte es una sentencia
que ha de cumplirse siempre

At the beginning and end of each day
  I know
that nothing should be missed
not thought
not my name's bloody scent
Everything keeps its shape
the afternoon and its sonata
the night and its trembling legs
Nonetheless
far from fate
a disturbance
floods my soul's well
death is a sentence
that must always be served

Tumä jama tumä pänis

maka wyä'jätzi'i popo'jäyä syi'upapä'yomo
tese maka yak' wisa'e te' kiskuy-sutkuy
käwänyi'ajupä jäyä'omoram
Tumä' jama
jameminä mij' nhkonuks' kuy'omoram
jäyä'istam maka' yajk' tajsa'ya'e mij' aknaka
popo' jäyä'jinh
maka' nhtyi'uki
       citoto'is jye'a
           nhwynapä' tzäki
makari' yajkere' mij' näyi'

Un día un hombre
regalará crisantemos a la mujer amada
y renacerá el odio-amor
que esconden las flores
Un día
recuérdalo en tus oraciones
flores cubrirán tu boca
con crisantemos
y serás
      hálito de cigarra
          átomo de silencio
también se borrará tu nombre

One day a man
will give the woman he loves
    chrysanthemums
and the hate-love that flowers hide
will be renewed
One day
remember this in your prayers
chrysanthemums will cover your mouth
and you will be
      a cigarette's smoke
          an atom of silence
and your name shall be erased

JESUKRISTO'IS JA' NYIÄJK'TYIÄJYA ÄJ' TZUMAMA'IS KYONUKSKUY

Äj' tzumama'is ja' myuspäkä' kastiya'ore
natzu' jyampä'ä nhkyomi'is nhkyonuks'kutyam
natzu' syi'aä' tumä naptzu'
jyampäukam yanhuku'is myusokyu'tyi'am
Äj' tzumama'is wyanh'jampana' jutzyi'e' ore'omorire'na
muspapä tä' tzamä'sawa'jinh
tese' kujtne'pyana eyapä' nhkomi'is wyinanh'omoram
tese'na konukspa 'tzyi'okoyjinh ni'ijse
Jesukristo'is ja' myajna kyonujks'kuy
te' yore äj' nhtzumama'isnyi'e
nyiä' ijtuna' pomarrosas yoma'ram
tese' sunhkpana' tumä' matza
nhwyränh'omoram watpasenaka'
San Mikel Arkangelis ja' myajna' kyonuks'kuy
äj' tzumama'is kyonuks'kuy wenenh'omo yatzyi'onhkuy'tena'
jukis'tyit numpana' tese' poyajpana te' toya'ram
patzoke wejpana' tese' te' sunhkä mitana' yänhkuy'kämä
Te' yänhkuy'kyämärike pänayaju' kuyay'yune'ram

JESUCRISTO NO ENTENDIÓ JAMÁS LOS RUEGOS DE MI ABUELA

Mi abuela nunca aprendió español
tuvo miedo del olvido de sus dioses
tuvo miedo de despertar una mañana
sin los prodigios de su prole en la memoria
Mi abuela creía que sólo en zoque
se podía hablar con el viento
pero se arrodillaba ante los santos
y oraba con fervor más que nadie
Jesucristo nunca la escuchó
la lengua de mi abuela
tenía el aroma de las pomarrosas
y el brillo de una estrella
le nacía en los ojos cuando cantaba
San Miguel Arcángel nunca la escuchó
los ruegos de mi abuela a veces eran
    blasfemias
jukis'tyit decía y los dolores cesaban
patzoke gritaba y el tiempo se detenía bajo
    su cama
En esa misma cama parió a sus siete hijos

JESUS NEVER UNDERSTOOD MY GRANDMOTHER'S PRAYERS

My grandmother never learned Spanish
was afraid of forgetting her gods
was afraid of waking up in the morning
having forgotten the wonders of her
    lineage
My grandmother believed that you could
    only
talk to the wind in Zoque
but she kneeled before the saints
and prayed with more fervor than anyone
Jesus never listened to her
my grandmother's tongue
smelled like rose apples
and her eyes lit up when she sang
with the brilliance of a star.
Archangel Michael never listened to her
my grandmother's prayers were sometimes
    blasphemies
jukis'tyit she said and the pain stopped
patzoke she yelled and time paused
    beneath her bed
In that same bed she birthed her seven
    children

WANHJAMPATZI YOM'NHKOMI NYIÄYI'PÄIS
SOLEDAD

Yom'nhkomi mij' näyipäis Soledad
yäkpa äjtzy'kämä'
wäkä nhtä' sijka' äj' yosyi'kuy
myita' äj' jäsmäjk wäkä' nhtä' nhtanjä' äj' nhtzokoy
Te' jaya'uneram mäjtzä'yajpapäna' äjtzyinh yenh'yajum
yäti' yajk' omyajpa' ero'ina
yuj'kyajpa taka'nyiä' jinam myapasyiäya'e
teramte' yajk' kayajpapäis jyara, ji' wyanh'jamya'epäis nhtä' nhkomi
Te' yom'uneram yenh'yajkeruri'
yäti' yomoramte' tzyiä'pyajpapäis yuka'käjsi yune'ram
pyatzoke'uneram
yomoram' kyojä'yajpapäis jyaya'ram kayajupä eya'najsomoram
Yom'nhkomi mij' näyipäis Soledad
mpäjku' äj' nhtzokoy mij' masanh'täjkse'
te'masanh'täjk'tike jurä' mäjtzä'yutzi te' une'jinhtam
te' une'ram jinam' mapä' nhtä' tujk'wyru'rame'

MI VIRGEN SE LLAMA
SOLEDAD

Oh, Virgen de la Soledad
te acuestas a mi lado
para echarme en cara la tristeza de mi
 oficio
me embistes por la espalda como buena
 enemiga
Los niños que jugaron conmigo ya no son
 niños
ahora se inyectan heroína
beben cerveza y nunca más sueñan
son los parricidas y golpeadores de Dios
Las niñas también crecieron
ahora son mujeres llevando sobre la
 espalda
a sus hijos bastardos
mujeres que lloran por sus hombres
 muertos en la frontera
Oh, Virgen de la Soledad
hiciste de mi paria corazón tu templo
el mismo templo donde jugué con aquellos
 niños
que nunca más volveremos a ser

MY VIRGIN'S NAMED FOR
SOLITUDE

Oh, Virgen de la Soledad
you bend toward me
to rub my face in the sorrow of my calling
you attack me behind my back like a
 worthy foe
The boys who played with me are no
 longer boys
now they shoot heroin
chase beers instead of dreams
The girls grew up too
now they are women toting
their bastard children on their backs
women who cry for their men dead at the
 border
Oh, Virgen de la Soledad
you made a temple of my pariah heart
the same temple where I played with those
 children
we'll never be again

NHTÄ' NHTZAMÄ ORE' SASYAPYÄ TIRE'

Tzätzä' Ore'yomo
Yom'une, nhkya'e' pekapäis'tzyokoy,
yomo jyamopi'apä'is kotzojkomo'ram.
Atzi' Ore'pät
Jaya'une,
ejtzpapä' nhka'e,
nijpapä pät'.
Yä' jama'omo
makapäre' nhtzyap'tziranhtä'i
te' kojama makapä'jinh
Nhtä' wyjtame yä' nasakopajkäjsi.
Tzätzä' Ore'yomo
mijsyi'koroya yä kojama tyotpapä'is toya',
yä' kojama yajk' pajkpapä'is te' sutkuy.
Atzi' Ore'pät
mijsyi'koroya pämi'äyupä'kojama,
kojama yajk' tenh'papäis tuj',
yajk' pajkpapäis te' ninhkä' teserike te' pakak.
Yom'une
Jaya'une,
mijsyi'koroyaram yä' sanhkä,
mijsyi'koroyaram yä' musokyuy.

SER ZOQUE ES UN PRIVILEGIO

Hermanita zoque
Ore'yomo,
niña de corazón antiguo,
mujer espíritu de los cerros.
Hermanito zoque
Ore'pät,
niño danzante,
hombre que cultivas la tierra.
Hoy es el día para nombrar la sagrada
   palabra,
hoy es el día para designar al animal
que los protegerá en esta tierra.
Hermanita zoque,
para ti la fuerza ante el dolor,
para ti el poder ante el deseo.
Hermanito zoque
que tu nagual sea poderoso,
resistente a la lluvia, resistente al calor y al
   frío.
Hermanita zoque,
Hermanito zoque,
para ustedes el resplandor,
para ustedes la sabiduría.

TO BE ZOQUE IS A PRIVILEGE

Little Zoque sister
Ore'yomo,
ancient-hearted girl
mountain-spirit woman.
Little Zoque brother
Ore'pät,
dancer boy
man who tills the earth.
Today the sacred words are invoked,
today your animal protector
will be revealed.
Little Zoque sister
for you the strength to face pain,
for you the power to face desire.
Little Zoque brother
may your nagual be powerful
immune to rain, heat, and cold.
Little Zoque sister,
Little Zoque brother,
for both of you,
radiance and wisdom.

PÄJKINH'TZYOKI'UY' MOKAYA'PÄTKOROYA

Mokaya jaya'une yäjse'
mij' mpäkinh'ntzyi'okpa' nasakopaj'käjsi.
Yäki' ijtyaju yä' tzama'ram
juwä nhtä' anhuku'istam
oyu' yajk pujksya'e tyiämpu'
yäti' mijtzanhte makapä nyipi'pänh'aje'.
Yäki' ijtyi'aju yä' poporampä jojpaktam
yuj'kyajumä nä'
mumu' oyupäis' nhwyjtyi'a'e Ajway'
yäti muspa ya'ä' mij' nhkänh'tätzä
yä' näjinh'.
Yaki' ijtyi'aju yä' kopänhtam'
yajk' tzinh'yajpapä'is' te' tzama',
tejinhte makapä wyij'tum'nhtame'.
Mijte mapä' nhkokene' yä' nasakopajk
Tzama'komis maka yajk mapasyi'äyi'
Pi'okpatzyuwe'is maka nhky'äwäni'
Kotzäjkpänis maka mpiä'mitzi'i.
¿tiya muspa mij' ntzajka' yaju'kamäjtzi
uka nitiyä" ji' nhtyi'ame yä' nasakopajkäjsi?

RECIBIMIENTO DEL HOMBRE MOKAYA

Mokaya, amado niño,
así te recibo en esta tierra.
Aquí están las montañas
donde nuestros ancestros
esparcieron las semillas,
ahora, serás tú el sembrador.
Aquí están los límpidos manantiales˙
que hemos bebido
desde siempre en Ajway',
ahora, saciarás también tu sed.
Aquí están las plantas y los animales
que embellecen el bosque, ahora,
    caminarás entre ellos.
Serás su protector,
el dueño del monte te guiará en sueños,
la señora del Volcán te esconderá de tus
    enemigos,
el dueño del cerro será tu fortaleza.
¿Qué más puedo heredarte
si nada perdura en la tierra?

RECEPTION FOR A MOKAYA MAN

Mokaya, beloved boy,
I welcome you to this land.
Here are the mountains
where our ancestors
scattered seeds;
you are the sower now.
Here are the limpid springs
that we have always
drunk in Ajway;
you will slake your thirst here now.
Here are the plants and animals that bring
    beauty
to our forest; now you will walk among
    them.
You will be their protector,
the Forest Guardian will guide you in your
    dreams,
the Volcano Queen will hide you from
    your enemies,
the Mountain King will be your strength.
What more can I bequeath you
if nothing on earth will last?

PÄJKINH'TZYI'OKYUY MOKAYA'YOMO'KOROYA

Mokaya sunhtäjupä yom'une,
masänh'äjkyutyi'e mij' mpänajkuy,
Ipstäjk'kujkmäpäre ne' tzyunh'u,
ne' nejnayaju' Mä'ä'pänis'tzyi'ameram
teserike Oko'sawas' pyämi'.
Mijtene' te' wäpyä'kojama oyupä nyiä' ijtyi'a'e
winarampä' tzame'yomo'istam yäki Ajwaymä.
Wenerampä näpyajpa makanh' tä' yajpärame
nhtä tzap'tampapä'is ore', jinamum ma' tä' kenh'tame nasakopajkäjsi.
Mijtzi' yom'une
maka' tyajk kopujkstame'.
Nhtä' näpinh'tzajtyi'am masanh pijstinh'sepäre'
mapäre' tyi'one' makasenh'omo iri' yä' nasakopajk.

RECIBIMIENTO DE LA MUJER MOKAYA

Mokaya, amada niña,
honrados estamos con tu llegada,
vienes de las profundidades de Ipstäjk,
traes el saludo de Los hombres Rayo,
y la fuerza de Oko'sawa.
Eres el espíritu armónico
de las primeras abuelas de Ajway'.
Algunos dicen que ya no habrá Mokayas,
que estamos condenados al exterminio.
Pero tú, mi niña,
vienes a renovarnos.
Nuestra sangre es como la sagrada ceiba
que perdurará hasta que viva la tierra.

RECEPTION FOR A MOKAYA WOMAN

Mokaya, beloved girl,
we are honored by your arrival,
you come from the inner world,
carrying the Thunderbolt Men's greeting,
and the Wind Goddess's powers.
You are the harmonious spirit
of Ajway's ancestor-women.
Some say there will be no more Mokayas,
that we are condemned to extinction.
But you, my child,
come to renew us.
Our blood runs in the veins of the ceiba
that will live as long as the earth.

AJ' JARA'IS TZI'UPÄ'

Jaräkmana' äj' ame'
äj' jara'is nhwäjätzi'utzi
tumä putzyi'jonhtzyi
mojtupä' tzapas'kenejinh
tumä' jonhtzyi' wat'papäna'
tome' äj' aknakämä
isanh'ntzipapäsna' mumu ti'is nyiäyiram
we', we', we'
ore', ore' ore'
wik', wik' wik'.
Jaräkmana' äj ame'
tumä putzyi'jonhtzyi'is isanhntzi'utzi jujtzye' wanä' ore'omo
isanhtzi'utzi' jujtzyi'e irä' yä' nasakopajkäjsi
teserike nhkomujsa tzajpijs'yore.
Uka' sajpa mij' nhtzame, wäpare yajk' tukä'
Uka nhkyomej'kopya nhtzaku'tzyipa' mij' nhwyt.
Tekoroya tä' näjmatyanh'täjpa Ore'pät, Ore'yomo.
Nhtä' äjtyamanhnte nhtyajk' tzinh'tampapä'is te' tzame.
Temä' tza'momo yenhpa' te' wewe'
tumä putzyi'jäyä mojtupä' tzapas'kene'jinh,
tumä jonhtzyi' watpapä'
teserike tä' isanhn'tzipapäis jujtzyi'e tä' wanä'
we', we' we'
ore, ore, ore
wik, wik wik.

MI PADRE ME DIO UN REGALO

Cuando niña
mi padre me trajo un regalo,
me dio un pájaro amarillo
con manchitas naranjas,
un pajarillo que cantaba
muy cerca de mi boca
y me mostraba los nombres de las cosas.
We, we, we
ore, ore, ore
wik, wik, wik.
Cuando niña,
un pájaro amarillo me enseñó a cantar en
    zoque,
me anticipó al mundo,
me mostró el lenguaje del universo.
Si empeñas tu palabra, debes ennoblecerla.
Si mientes, deshonras tu existencia.
Por eso nos llaman Ore'pät, Ore'yomo.
Somos los hombres y mujeres de la
    palabra.
Allá en la montaña crece el wewe,
una flor amarilla con manchas naranjas,
un pájaro que canta
y enseña a los zoques a cantar
we, we, we
ore, ore, ore
wik, wik, wik.

MY FATHER GAVE ME A GIFT

When I was young
my father brought me a gift,
a yellow bird
with orange spots,
a little bird that sang
right by my mouth
and taught me the names of things.
We, we, we
ore, ore, ore
wik, wik, wik.
When I was young,
a yellow bird taught me to sing in Zoque,
opened up the world to me,
showed me the universe's language.
If you give your word, you must honor it.
If you lie, you dishonor yourself.
That is why we are called Ore'pät,
    Ore'yomo.
We are men and women of our word.
There in the mountains the wewe grows,
a yellow flower with orange spots,
a bird that sings
and teaches the Zoques to sing
we, we, we
ore, ore, ore
wik, wik, wik.

WE'WE'

Te' Nhkirawa'is näjmayutzi',
nhki'a'e mina' yäki', nhtä' nhtzajma
jujtzyi'e nä' yospa' mij' wewe'
Tese nhkämetzutzi, jujtzyi'a mujspa nhtä ijsä'
winanh'kene'omo
tzokoyis nhtyi'osyi'kuy.
Wewe', wewe' wewe'
nä' ijtukna' majkäs'täjkay'poya
äjn apä'is nejnayutzi tumä' wewe'
te' jäyä' nhtä' tzaptzunh'tampäpä'jinh.
Wewe', wewe' wewe'
nhki'a'e nhtä' ma'tzyi'ä' mij' jäyä'
neri' yajk' wajna'tyi'oyajkeru' äj uneram.
Jine' atzy'ä, jin musji' ma'ä.
Uj' nyi'atzyokoy'aju nhki'a'e, nhtä' tzajma jujtzyi'e nhtzampa mij jäyä'.
Jine' atzy'ä, jin musji' ma'ä.
Jujtzyi'a mujspa nhtä ijsä'
winanh'kene'omo
tzokoyis nhtyosyi'kuy.

WEWE

El nhkirawa me dijo:
niña, ven aquí y explícame
cómo funciona tu dichoso Wewe.
¿Acaso está permitido al ojo humano
descubrir a primera vista
cómo funciona el corazón?
Wewe, wewe, wewe.
Cuando tenía 9 meses,
mi abuelo me trajo el wewe,
la plantita que hace florecer la palabra
de los Mokayas.
Wewe, wewe, wewe.
Niña, véndeme tu flor,
también quiero que mis hijos canten al sol.
No, señor, no se puede.
No seas mala, niña, dime cuánto vale esa
   flor.
No, señor, no se puede.
¿Acaso está permitido al ojo humano
descubrir a primera vista
cómo funciona el corazón?

WEWE

The Nhkirawa told me:
little girl, come here and explain
how your wonderful wewe works.
Is the human eye really allowed
to learn at first glance
how the heart works?
Wewe, wewe, wewe.
When I was nine months old,
My grandfather brought me a wewe,
the little plant that makes the Mokaya
language bloom.
Wewe, wewe, wewe.
Little girl, sell me your flower,
I want my children to sing to the sun, too.
No, Mister, that's impossible.
Don't be a bad girl, tell me how much that
   flower costs.
No, Mister, that's impossible.
Is the human eye really allowed
to learn at first glance
how the heart works?

TZOKO'TZYAME

Äj' apä'is näjmayutzi:
Anhuku'is tzajkatyi'anh'täjupä ore'tzamere.
yäti ¿isaj' yanhkasäpya te' tzame?
Yäti sunh'nhtäjpapä unhtzame're,
yajk' tzajkya'ä tyiäwäsntyojsanh'tam.
Tum'jama äj' apä' oyu' nämi'
ore'pänhtam wäpä' najsomo're tä' ijta'upä,
jiksekanhte' mytyi'ajupä te' mineru'ram
sutupure nyiä' maki'a'ä sunh'yajpapä ti'ram tzyajinh'nhtuku.
Aj apä'is tzyampapäna jinte'na sunh'yajpapä'tiram
ore'tzame'rena,
te Ore' yajk jäyäpya'päis te' nhkipsokyuy
teserike te' tzokoy, te Ore' tzinhpapä
wewe'jinh.
Te Wewe' yajk' popa'päis
sasatyi'ampä tzame unes' yaknakomo'ram,
tzame jontzyi'wanejse nhtä manhpapä
nimeke yajk' kasäjpapä'is te' nasakopajk'.
Tekoroya jinh' näjktyiä'tyianh'täyi nhkirawa'jinhtam
Testam nhkyps'syajpa' nhkyopajkinh'tam
äjtam nhkyps'tampatzi äj nhtzokoy'jinhtam.

126   Mikeas Sánchez

PENSAR CON EL CORAZÓN

Mi abuelo me dijo:
Los zoques somos herederos de la palabra,
pero ¿a quién le importa ahora la palabra?
La mayoría prefiere mentir,
despojar a otros de sus pequeños tesoros.
Un día mi abuelo aseguró
que en nuestras tierras abundaban
   riquezas,
entonces vinieron los mineros
y quisieron llevarse hasta las piedras.
Mi abuelo hablaba del tesoro
de poseer la palabra,
de hacer florecer en el pensamiento
y en el corazón, la maravillosa plantita
que se llama wewe.
El wewe que inspira a los niños
a expulsar florecitas dulces de sus bocas,
imitaciones de mirlo o de cardenal
que llenan la tierra de júbilo.
Por eso nunca podremos entendernos con
   los nhkirawas.
Ellos piensan con la cabeza
y nosotros pensamos con el corazón.

THINKING WITH OUR HEARTS

My grandfather told me:
We Zoques are inheritors of the word,
but who cares about words now?
Most prefer to lie,
stealing the earth's treasures.
My grandfather said
that our lands were filled with riches,
and so the miners came
and wanted to steal every last stone.
My grandfather spoke of the treasure
of making language bloom
in our thoughts and our hearts,
of our marvelous plant called wewe.
The wewe inspires children to
spill sweet flowers from their mouths,
mimicking Cardinal and Blackbird
who fill our lands with joy.
This is why the Nhkirawas never
   understand us.
They think with their heads
and we think with our hearts.

WÄKÄ' JANA TYI'UJANÄMÄ' NIJP'PYAJPAK

Uka mpyäjkpa tujis' mij' nhyosykuy'omo,
Uka ji' mujsi' ma' mpyajtzyiäkä',
Uka ji' tyiä'tzi' mij' nhtuku',
Uka te' tzunhkäis yajk mujapya mij' nhtäjkis'nyi'ajs
Uka te' kä'pi' tzoko, ji' nyi'eme,
Uka' te' ontyi'ujis yajk tuj'yapi'a mij' juktäjk'
Uka kejkpa tuj' sawa nhkyo'räjkajpapä' jama'omo,
Uka pämipä' tujis' nyi'ajapya mij' nipi',
Uka tuj'sawa'is nyi'ajapya mij' nhkupkuy,
Uka' mpämipä tujis' nyä' manh'japya mij' ntäjk',
Uka mäjapä' tuj'sawa'is nyiä' manh'japya mij' nhtäjkis'yajy'.
Tesepä tiyä toyare', atzi' Mokaya,
Nasakopajkis' nhkyomusapya mij' nhtoya',
tekoroya ji' nhwyiä' yatzyi'äyä' te' tuj',
ijtu tumä toya' jene' nhtyajk topyapä,
nimeke mäjapa, tere' te Tuj'Sawas nhkisä' nyijp'pyajpapä' jama.

PARA QUE NO LLUEVA EL DÍA DE TU ENTIERRO

Si un aguacero te sorprende en el trabajo,
si no puedes salir de paseo,
si la ropa no se seca,
si la gotera moja tu piso,
si la leña es demasiado húmeda para arder,
si la llovizna arruina tu fogón,
si cae una tormenta el día de tu boda,
si un aluvión destruye tu cosecha,
si una tromba devasta tu ciudad,
si la inundación arrasa tu casa,
si el huracán te deja sin techo.
Todo esto es aterrador, hermano Mokaya,
y Nasakopajk' conoce tu sufrimiento,
pero nunca debes blasfemar contra la
    lluvia,
porque nada puede ser más triste para un
    Mokaya
que la furia de Tuj'sawa el día de su
    entierro.

SO IT WON'T RAIN ON YOUR BURIAL DAY

If a downpour catches you off guard at
    work,
if you can't go out for a walk,
if the laundry doesn't dry,
if a leak soaks the floor,
if the firewood is too damp to catch,
if drizzle wrecks the cooking fire,
if rain falls on your wedding day,
if a rising river ruins your harvest,
if a cyclone destroys your city,
if the flood razes your house,
if the hurricane leaves you roofless.
This is all terrifying, Zoque brother,
and Nasakopajk' knows your suffering,
but you must never curse the rain,
because nothing would be sadder for a
    Mokaya
than Storm God's fury on your burial day.

WENHTI'

Sapa' te' mäja'ju'ki,
syukpa' te' najs,
yaku'ajkyajpa mäjarampä syaja'ram
sirijtpa käsi'anhkas, syi'ukyajpasenh'omo te' ona'ram
Syi'asa'ajkuy mäjapäre
tekoroya kasäjpa myojkpa
yä' nasakopajk.

Sapa' te pät, mayapa',
nhtyi'a'tzyiä'pya yijtkuy, ja' nyiä' irä'anhkä saja',
maka'ankä' ya'e' syi'asa'ajkuy, maka'ankä atzyi'pä'aje'.

Te' wäpä' wenhti' nhtä nhkomi'koroya
ju'kiste nhkyonukskuy.
Te' wäpä' wenhti' nhtä' nhkomi'koroya.
pujtpa' ji' wyewenek' te' pät.

OFRENDA

Despierta el zopilote rey
y besa la tierra, extiende sus formidables
   alas
y vuela hasta bailar con las nubes.
Su mayor encanto
es su maestría
para limpiar el mundo.

Despierta el hombre y sufre,
maldice por haber nacido sin alas
y con una belleza tan fugaz.

No hay mejor ofrenda para los dioses
que la reverencia del zopilote.
No hay mejor ofrenda para los dioses
que el silencio del hombre.

GIFT

The vulture king wakes up
and kisses the earth, stretches his
   impressive wings
and flies until he dances with the clouds.
His greatest gift
is his mastery
in cleaning the earth.

Humans wake up and suffer,
cursing for having been born wingless
and with such ephemeral beauty.

There is no greater gift to the gods
than the vulture's reverence.
There is no greater gift to the gods
than human silence.

TUMÄ UNE' MAPASYIÄPYA

Tumä' tzapajs'jonhtzyi' mapasyiä'pyak,
mytyi'ajpa nhtä' nhkomi'ram.
Tumä une' mapasyiä'pyak,
kasäyajpa nhtä' nhkomi'ram.
Te mapasyi' tzapas'jontzyis'nyi'e jinhte' unes' myapasyi',
tese' myesyi'käyi' nhnyiä' ijtyi'aju' te' nasakopajkis myusoki'uy.
Wäkä nhtä ispäjktämä' wäpä' ijtkuy
syi'upapäre' nhtä' nhtzajktamä
wäkä te' tzapas'jonhtzyi syi'rirä jujtzyi'enh'omo syi'upa' nyi'ekä.
Wäkä nhtä' ispäjktamä' wäpä' ijtkuy
syi'upapäre' nhtä' majnatyi'amä te' une'is myapasyiäpi'apä.

UN NIÑO SUEÑA

Un águila sueña
y los dioses se acercan.
Un niño sueña
y los dioses se regocijan.
El sueño del águila no es el sueño del niño,
pero ambos guardan la pureza del mundo.
Para que el bosque siga en armonía,
hay que dejar al águila
volar libremente.
Para que la tierra mantenga la paz,
hay que saber escuchar el sueño del niño.

A CHILD DREAMS

An eagle dreams
and the gods approach.
A child dreams
and the gods rejoice.
The eagle's dream isn't the child's dream,
but both contain the purity of the world.
For the forest to thrive,
we must let the eagle
fly free.
To sustain peace on earth,
we must know how to listen to children's
    dreams.

JUJTZYI'E NHTÄ WÄPÄ TZAMAPÄNH'AJÄ

Simón, äj' atzyipä'jara sutu' wäpä tzamapänh'ajä,
kyomujsu kastiya'ore
teserike mumupä nhtä' nhkomis' nyiäyiram.
Ejtzu' masanh'nhtäjkis wynanh'omo
teserike' mpyäkinh'tzyoku' sijkpa' te' näyä'yäki'uy.
Äj› atzyipä'jara'is nyiä' ijtayuna' tzapas'Mää'is pyä'mi,
Nhkyo'jama kak'tena'.
Äj atzyipä'jara ketkäkätpapä'pänhtena
te'is muspana' tyak' tzoka tzyi'ame'jinhtam.
Te' sutu' wäpä' tzamapänh'ajä,
myuspäjku jujtzyi'e yajk' yosa' te' käjtz'täjkuy',
teserike' nhkyenh'tuyu' te' nhkyrawa'is'nyi'o'a'ram.
Äj› atzyipä'jara musopyapä' pänh'tena,
te'is muspana' nyiä' tzapi'a'ä pyeka'nhkomi'ram.
Äj atzyipä'jara sutu' wäpä tzamapänh'ajä,
tese'ja' myujsä jujtzyi'e tzyiäkä.

CÓMO SER UN BUEN SALVAJE

Mi abuelo Simón quiso ser un buen salvaje,
aprendió castilla
y el nombre de todos los santos.
Danzó frente al templo
y recibió el bautismo con una sonrisa.
Mi abuelo tenía la fuerza del Rayo Rojo
y su nagual era un tigre.
Mi abuelo era un poeta
que curaba con las palabras.
Pero él quiso ser un buen salvaje,
aprendió a usar la cuchara,
y admiró la electricidad.
Mi abuelo era un chamán poderoso
que conocía el lenguaje de los dioses.
Pero él quiso ser un buen salvaje,
aunque nunca lo consiguió.

HOW TO BE A GOOD SAVAGE

My grandfather Simón wanted to be a
   good savage,
he learned Spanish,
and all the saints' names.
He danced before the church
and was baptized with a smile.
My grandfather had the force of Red
   Thunder
and his nagual was a tiger.
My grandfather was a poet
who healed with words.
But he wanted to be a good savage,
learned to eat with a spoon,
and the Nhkirawa's electric lamps
   impressed him.
My grandfather was a powerful shaman
who spoke the gods' language.
He wanted to be a good savage,
but he never quite learned how.

TE' MEKE

Ji' nhkiänatzä'yoyepä' papynyi'omo'is
syi'nawajku nhwyt'
tese' nhki'omusku'päjki'aju sone' tzame'ram
jiksekanhte myatyajupä te' mä'ä'pät teserike te' tuj'pät,
kora'ayajpa' ne' myanyi'aju'ankä yom'nhtzame'ram
sutu' nyi'ujkya'ä te' tzame'ram
wäkä' yajk' wyruya'ä jojpajk'omoram,
   tzajp'omoram,
      matza'omoram,
        kotzäjk'omoram,
          tzu'omoram teserike jama'omoram
tese' mytyi'aju äj' nhtzätzä' tzeke'ram
äj' nhtzätzä' tompijtz'tam
teis'tam nyi'etyaju kyowa'ram, syusku'tyam
jiksekante te' sawa'pät te' mä'ä'pät
poksyajupä wäkä' nhkyämanäya'ä
te' sasapyä' wane' pujtupä jiksekpä' tzayi'omo.

EL FESTÍN

La muchacha subversiva que soy
rompió las amarras
y cayó con furia sobre cada palabra
    prohibida.
Entonces vinieron los dioses del trueno y
    de la lluvia
alegando la imprudencia de lo femenino,
quisieron capturar las palabras
y regresarlas de nuevo a los ríos
      a los cielos
           a las estrellas
                a los volcanes
                    a la noche y al día,
pero vinieron también las hermanas
    tortugas
y las hermanas tuzas
con sus instrumentos de percusión y de
    viento,
entonces los dioses de la lluvia y el trueno
se sentaron a escuchar
la hermosa sonata que salió aquella tarde.

FEAST

The subversive young woman I am
broke barriers
and fell furiously on every forbidden word.
Then the rain and thunder gods showed up
irritated by such feminine recklessness,
tried to trap my words
and return them to the rivers
      to the skies
           to the stars
                to the volcanoes
                    to night and day,
but our sisters the turtles and gophers
also showed up with their flutes and drums
and so the rain and thunder gods
sat down to enjoy
the sweet sonata unleashed that afternoon.

MAPASYIÄPYATZI YÄJKPÄ'WAKAS

Nhkotzampatzi te' jama jurä pänajumä',
te' tuj' poya
jurä' te' oko'tzyi'uwe'is jajkayutzi äj' nhtunu'tzajy
wäkä nyipä' täjkä'josmäjk.
äj› nhtzu'mayi'ram
teserike' mumu' äj yom'nhtäwäram
uma' ayaju te' jama'omo
ni'is ja' syunä' tzyi'amä' nitiyä'
ni'is ja' kyotzamä äj nhkojama yäjkpä'kopänh
Tese' nhkomus'päjkyajutzi te' yom'yosyku'y.
Näjmaya'jutzi jana' nhkämetza jujtzyepäre' te' etze',
te' wane' teserike te' matza'is tzyi'ameram.
Tese' papinyi'omo'ajutzi popyasenh'omo mäja'kupkuy'omoram,
tese yomo'ajutzi mapasyä'pyasenh'omo yäjkpä'wakas.

SOÑANDO CON UN TORO NEGRO

Hablo de mi nacimiento,
aquel día lluvioso
en que la partera cortó mi cordón
  umbilical
para enterrarlo detrás de la casa.
Mi madre,
mi abuela
y todo mi linaje femenino
enmudecieron ese día.
Nadie quiso decir nada,
nadie habló de mi nagual corazón de toro
  negro.
Y aprendí los oficios de mi género
y me fue prohibida la danza,
la música y el lenguaje de las estrellas.
Y me hice muchacha corriendo por las
  urbes
y me hice mujer soñando con un toro
  negro.

DREAMING OF A BLACK BULL

I speak of my birth,
that rainy day
the midwife cut my umbilical cord
to bury it behind our house.
My mother,
grandmother,
and all my female ancestors
fell silent that day.
No one wanted to say anything,
no one spoke of my nagual the black bull.
So I learned the duties of my gender
and that dancing,
music, and celestial language were
  forbidden.
I came of age in the city and became
a woman dreaming of a black bull.

PISTINH

Pistinh masanh'äyupä,
Apus'yunestam
mij' anhkasä'tyi'ampatzi yä' nasakopajkäsi,
jampärantä'jutzi
totzyiäjk'tanhtä'jutzi,
ijtu' syutyajupä'is tä' yajatyamä nhtä' jameram,
ijtu' syutyajupä'is tä totzyiäjk'katyamä nhtä' nhtzokotyam,
ijtu' syutyajupä'is tyajk jampäramä nhtä mpämi'ram.

Mäja'kujy tyotzyiäj'kyajupä
totzyiäjk'tanhtäjuse' äjtam ore'pät, teserike ore'yomoram,
nhtä' isanhtziramä' jutzyi'e mapasyätyamä wina'ijtkuy'omojse,
jujtzyi'e mpat'wiruramä äj watzi'ram.

CEIBA

Sagrada Ceiba,
los descendientes de Saspalanki
honramos tu presencia sobre la tierra;
fuimos olvidados,
fuimos inmolados,
alguien sepultó nuestra memoria,
alguien enturbió nuestro corazón,
alguien quiso apagar nuestra llama.

Gran árbol mutilado
lo mismo que los ore'pät y las ore'yomo,
permítenos ahora soñar de nuevo
y encontrar nuestra raíz.

CEIBA

Sacred Ceiba,
we descendants of Saspalanki
honor your presence on earth;
we were forgotten,
we were sacrificed,
someone buried our memory,
someone roiled our hearts,
someone tried to smother our flame.

Great tree, maimed
as our Zoque ancestors were,
let us dream anew
and find our roots.

MÄJA KUPKUY'OMO SASPALANKIS'YUNERAM JÄTYI'AMPATZI

Ore'pät, Ore'yomo, Saspalankis'yuneram
nhkopikta'utzi' pänajtamä yä' nasakopajkäjsi,
äj nhkojamas'tam wyänh'pama te' 'pyeka'omoma,
nema' myujupä tzapas'najsis'yomoma,
kujy'omoma'ram, tanä'omoma'ram.
Tokotyi'a'upä' uneramätzyiä yä' mäja' kupkuy'omo'ram
totyi'rampä'uneram mye'tzyi'ajpäpä'is myapasyram
Tikoroya' nhwyrupa' mij' nhkupkuy'omo
-nhkyä'metzyajpa nhtä' yoskuy'tziyajpapä'is-
Tzäyä' yä' mäja'kupkuy'omo soka'une, tzäkä wäpä'tiyä,
¡wänä' mij' nhtuminh, ju'yä' mij' nhkarru!
¡juyä' mij motocikleta!
¿nhwyj'tyi'opa'a kosyitaksi mij' atzyipä'jara'se?
Tzäyä' yä' mäjakupkuy'omo papinyi'omo, tzäkä' wäpä'tiyä
Juyä' sunyityi'ampä asa',
sasatyi'ampä kä'ajk kejyapapä sunhpapä'kene'omo
¿Jinare' tza'ajkuy mesa' peka'asa mij' nhtzümayis'nyi'esepä?

Mäja kupkuy'omo Saspalankis'yuneram jätyi'ampatzi
tese' jowyjse' kasäjtampa kejkpak te' tuj'
tekoroya popya pujtampa wäkä yajk' mujtamä äj' nhwinh'tam
tese' yäki' ji' mpyuj'tyi'a'e joyjoye'ram.
Yä' mäja'räjktam ka'yajupäsere ijtyi'ajupä, ji' tzyapya'e.
Mäja kupkuy'omo Saspalankis'yuneram jätyi'ampatzi
tekoroya' wiru'rampak äj nhtäjk'omoram
kasäjpa' ejtztzyi'ajpa' äj' nhkojama'ram
ejtztzyi'ajpa' mäja' sunh'omojse'

LOS HIJOS DE SASPALANKI LLORAMOS EN LA GRAN CIUDAD

Los hijos de Saspalanki
elegimos nacer en esta tierra,
nuestro espíritu aún guarda su olor más
    antiguo,
aroma a tierra roja recién mojada,
olor a guarumo y madreselva.
Somos como niños extraviados en esta
    gran ciudad,
niñitos ciegos persiguiendo burbujas en el
    aire.
¿Para qué regresas a tu tierra?
preguntan los dueños del tiempo.
Quédate en la ciudad, muchacho, y sé
    alguien en la vida
¡Ahorra para tu carro!
¡Cómprate una motocicleta!
¿Acaso quieres caminar descalzo como tu
    abuelo?
Quédate en la ciudad, muchacha, y sé
    alguien en la vida,
cómprate el vestido de moda,
las zapatillas de las revistas.
¿Acaso no es vergüenza vestir como tu
    abuela?

Los hijos de Saspalanki lloramos en la
    Gran Ciudad,

SASPALANKI'S CHILDREN CRY IN THE BIG CITY

We children of Saspalanki
chose to be born in this land,
our spirit still guards its ancient scent,
aroma of red earth freshly wet,
smell of guarumo palm and honeysuckle.
We are like children lost in this big city,
blind babes chasing bubbles though the air.
Why return to your land?
ask the clock-watchers.
Stay here in the city, young man, and
    become somebody.
Save up for a car!
Buy a motorcycle!
Would you rather walk barefoot like your
    grandfather?
Stay here in the city, young lady, and
    become somebody,
buy a stylish dress,
high heels like in the magazines.
Isn't it embarrassing to dress like your
    grandmother?

We children of Saspalanki cry in the Big
    City
break into wild frenzy when we see the rain,
going out to soak ourselves as if we've lost
    our minds,

Yäki' yä' najsomo tä' tzaka'tyanhtäjupä nhtä' anhuku'istam,
yä' najsomo juwä' kasäjpa' tä' ijtampamä
juwä' *jana'ruminh*
mujspamä' tä' ijtamä.

nos volvemos locos de frenesí cuando
   vemos caer las lluvias,
salimos como desquiciados a mojarnos,
pero aquí no aparecen los duendes del
   bosque.
Los edificios son oscuras tumbas y no
   hablan.
Los hijos de Saspalanki lloramos en la
   Gran Ciudad,
por eso, cuando por fin volvemos a casa,
nuestro nagual baila enardecido,
baila como en los días de fiesta.

Aquí en esta tierra que nos legaron
   nuestros ancestros
      en esta tierra donde se puede ser feliz
     y también nunca llegar a
     ser alguien en la vida.

but here the forest spirits don't appear.
The buildings are dark, silent tombs.
We children of Saspalanki cry in the Big
   City,
and so, when we finally return home,
our nagual dances as if on fire,
dances as if at fiesta.

Here in this land
   our ancestors gave us
      in this land where we can be happy
     and never manage
     to be somebody.

SONERAMPÄTE

Minä' äj' najsomo,
netyi'a'ä mij' nhtänh'kutyi'am,
kakutzyiya'ä te' nä tyi'onh'yajpapä wakasis'tam,
yajk' ka'e'aya'ä te' jojpajktam,
tänh'ä'yä putzi mutpamä te' nä,
mutpamä nhtä' nkomi'is nhwyränhk nä'.
Anhku'makäya'ä äj' atzi'ram,
tzaptzi'ya'ä te' tuminh,
sasatyampä nhkirawa'yomo'ram,
te' sutkuy muspapä nhtä' juyä'.
Anhku'makäya'ä äj' nhzätzä'ram,
tzaptzi'ya'ä kowina'ajkuy,
tzajmaya'ä jujtzyi'ere' wäpyä
te' nhkirawa'ijtkuy.

Minä' äj' najsomo,
nijpya'ä mij' nhtänh'kutyi'am
nhtyi'aj'yajpapäis
te' kasäj'kyuytyam,
Nhtä' isanh'tziramä' te' toya, te yajk'syu'ijtkuy,
te' tujkuyis pyämi'.
Sonerampäte'
jinh' mij' natz'tame'

SOMOS MILLONES

Ven a mi tierra,
instala tus máquinas,
envenena los ríos que bebe el ganado,
contamina los manantiales,
llena de podredumbre el ojo de agua
y el ojo de Dios.
Engaña a mis hermanos,
ofréceles el pan y la codicia,
los placeres de la carne,
el amor que se oferta al mejor postor.
Soborna a mis hermanas,
promételes poder y riqueza,
háblales de las maravillas
del Primer Mundo.

Ven a mi tierra,
instala tus máquinas aniquiladoras
de ternura,
muéstranos el dolor y la desesperanza,
el impacto de las balas.
Somos millones
y no te tenemos miedo.

WE ARE MILLIONS ·

Come to my land,
install your machines,
poison the rivers our livestock drink,
contaminate the aquifers,
shove garbage into the spring
and God's face.
Trick my brothers,
offer them bread and greed,
the pleasures of the flesh,
love auctioned to the highest bidder.
Bribe my sisters,
promise them power and money,
tell them about the wonders
of the First World.

Come to my land,
install your peace-destroying
machines,
show us pain and despair,
bullet wounds.
We are millions
and we stand unafraid.

How to Be a Good Savage   147

NÄ'PYAJPA, MOKAYARAM MAKA' YAJPÄ'YA'E

Nä'pyajpa, Mokayaram maka' yajpä'ya'e.
Nasakopajkäjsi maka' anhkim'ya'e,
yajka'oyeram, numyajpapä.
Teis'tam nyi'etyajpa yajkuy' nhtä najs'omoram,
yajk' ko'tzawa'ayajpa mij' uneram' jowy'mätzik'jinhtam
nyi'ujmayajpa mij' oko'uneram
nhkyäma'näyapajk' jana'tzokopyä, jana'nhkojamapä' wane'
¿Jinhte' myu'sya'epä jujtzyi'e nhtä' äjtyi'am tä' tumurampäre'?
Wina' oyupänhte mytyi'ajkere' eyarampä,
oyupäis nhtyaj'tyi'oya'e nhtä' anhuku'is tzyi'ameram,
oyupäis nhkyäwänyi'a'e wiyunhsepä nhtä' ijtkutyam
wäkä' tese' nitumäpä' Mokaya'is myujsuna'
nhkyäma'näjyaya'ä nhtyiä'wäis tzyi'ameram.
Tesere' tä wyrura'upä' yajkuy'omopä,
pujtu' nhtä' näpinh'tzajy'omoram te' masanh'oreram,
tyajk pämi'päjktampapäis tumtum'jama,
tesere' nhtä' kopujks'tampapä' nhtä' äjtyi'am Mokaya'ram
¿Jinajkste jyampäya'epä
nhtä' nhkomis' 'pyä'miram?

DICEN QUE LOS MOKAYAS NOS EXTINGUIREMOS

Dicen que los Mokayas nos extinguiremos,
que Nasakopajk' será poseída
por mercenarios y ladrones.
Ellos traen su odio a nuestras tierras,
embrutecen a tus hijos con baratijas,
alejan a tus nietos
con su música que no tiene alma.
¿Acaso desconocen que somos uno sólo?
Antes vinieron otros,
y callaron nuestra palabra,
escondieron la luz de nuestra memoria
para que nunca un Mokaya pudiera
escuchar a sus hermanos.
Pero resurgimos del espanto,
del ADN brotó el Ore' sagrado,
cada vez más fuertes
cada vez más Mokayas.
¿Acaso desconocen
el poder de nuestros dioses?

THEY SAY THE MOKAYAS WILL GO EXTINCT

They say the Mokayas will go extinct,
that Nasakopajk' will be overrun
by robbers and mercenaries.
They bring their hate to our lands,
corrupt your children with trinkets,
estrange your grandchildren
with their soulless music.
Don't they know we're all one people?
Others came before,
and silenced our words,
hid the light of our memory
so that no Mokaya could
hear their sisters and brothers.
But we recovered from the terror,
our sacred language sprang from our
    DNA,
stronger than ever
more Mokayas than ever.
Don't they know
the power of our gods?

JUJTZYI'ERE'

Te' yajkuyis'nhkyowinastam, tä' näjmatyampa:
Mij' nhkaj'kapyatzi sone'ruminh'jinh
te' tzujtzipä' mij' nhtzajp,
mij' nhtzäjk'pujtapyatzi sasyapyä' ma'a'räjk
uka' nhtyajk' täjkäpya mij' nhkotzäjk'omoram.
Tumä'millon tzujtzirampä'ruminh
wäkä' jampä'ä jujtzyi'e kasäjyajpa mij' uneram
poyajpajk onyi'tyuj'omo.
Mokayas'tam mij' nhkosijk'katyampatzi' mij' nhtzame',
motzyi'rampä'uneis myusyi'ajpapänhte,
jujtzyi'e te' tuminh yatzyi'ä'yupä wakas'tinh'ajpa,
nhtä' nhkätpak te' Tzu'anh.
Mokayas'tam mij' nhkämetz'tampatzi' mijtam',
yajkuyis' nhkyowina'ram.
¿mij' panhku'omorampä' tuminh'jinh
mujspa'a yajk' wyru'jatyi'amä
Tzusnäpajkis' syi'ajsa'ajkuy?
¿Sonepä' mij' nhtuminh'jinhtam maka'a nhkä'rejtame
wäkä' nimojktamä te' tzajp' puspä'ukam?

¿CUÁNTO VALE?

Los amos de la barbarie nos dicen:
Te ofrezco una cuenta millonaria
a cambio de tu cielo azul,
te construyo un hermoso supermercado
a cambio de tus montañas.
Un millón de dólares
por la sonrisa de tus hijos
que corren bajo la lluvia.
Los Mokayas nos reímos de su ignorancia,
hasta los niños más pequeños
saben que la fortuna se convierte en boñiga
cruzando la línea del Tzu'anh
Los Mokayas les preguntamos a ustedes,
amos de la decadencia.
¿Una cuenta millonaria
será suficiente para devolverle
la alegría a nuestros muertos?
¿Con cuánto dinero alcanzará
para limpiar el alma de la tristeza?

WHAT IS IT WORTH?

Those masters of barbarity tell us:
I'll give you a millionaire's bank account
in exchange for your blue sky,
I'll build you a nice supermarket
in exchange for your mountains.
One million dollars
for your children's smiles
as they run in the rain.
We Mokayas laugh at their ignorance,
even the smallest children
know that money turns to dung
when you pass over to Tzu'anh
We Mokayas ask you,
the masters of destruction.
Is a millionaire's bank account
enough to bring back
the laughter of our dead?
How much money will it take
to cleanse sadness from the soul?

TÄ' MOKAYA'RAMTE

Tä' näjmatyanh'täjpa tzamapänh'tam,
nhtä nhko'ontampa'ankä Nasakopajk
¿Tipä unes' nhkyotzok'tyi'opa te' yajka'oye,
makapä'is tyotzyiäjke' jäsikam te' myayi?
Äj'tamte Mokaya'ram,
Nijptampapä'is te' mojk'.
Jinhte' äjtam yatzyi'tzamapäntam,
Jinhte' äjtam te' ji' myusoya'epä'.
Nhkomustampatzi' jojpajkis yore'ram
                teserike tzamas'tzyi'ameram.
Äj'tamte' mij' ya'e ji' tzyi'okepä,
Äj'tamte te' musoki'uy ne' jokupä.
Mina' atzi' nhkirawa,
Maka' mij' isanh'tzirame' te wane' ji nhtä' jampä'ipä.
Mina tzätzä nhkyrawa,
Mijtz'koroya te' musoki'uy wäkä' jana nhtyi'a'ä mij' sasa'ajkuy.

SOMOS MOKAYAS

Nos llaman indios
por defender a Nasakopajk'
¿acaso un hijo ayudaría al verdugo
en ofensa de su madre?
Somos Mokayas,
sembradores de maíz.
No somos los salvajes,
no somos los incivilizados.
Comprendemos el lenguaje de los ríos
          y de las montañas.
Somos la herida que te sangra,
somos la respuesta a tu vacío.
Ven, hermano blanco,
te enseñaremos el canto que jamás se
    olvida.
Ven, hermana blanca,
te daremos el secreto de la belleza infinita.

WE ARE MOKAYAS

They call us Indians
for defending Nasakopajk'
but what child would help the executioner
rather than his mother?
We are Mokayas,
sowers of maize.
We aren't savages,
we aren't uncivilized.
We understand the language of rivers
          and hills.
We are the wound that will not heal,
we are the answer to your emptiness.
Come, white brother,
we will teach you a song you must
    remember.
Come, white sister,
we will give you the secret to the sublime.

MOKAYA, KÄMANÄ'

Wenenh'omo yäjkpä'poyo'
mita' nhtä' mapasyi'omopä
wäkä' tä' kajka' Nasakopajkis'nhkyene.
Pakujk'tzujk'iste tzyi'ame',
te' yajka'oye'is' nhtyäjk'omopäre pujt'pa te' tzame,
teram' te' kowa'patyi'ajupä'
makapäre' jä'ya'e' mumu'jama,
teram' te' toya'isyi'ajpapäis makapäre' myetzyi'a'e
jujtzyi'e 'yanh'kumakä'ya'ä, wäkä ma' pa'tyaä'.
Kämanä' mijtzi, sokapä'mokaya
Pakujk'tzujk jäyäre ja' nyi'ä iräpäis'yomoma,
toyare' ji' nhtyi'a'epä.
Kämanä' mijtzi papinyi'omopä Mokaya,
Pakujk'tzujk najste'
jurä' jinam musimä tä' nhwyruä Nasakopaj'käjsi.

ESCUCHA, MOKAYA

A veces un fragmento de polvo negro
nos llega desde el sueño
y cambia el color del mundo.
Es el mensaje de Pakujk'tzujk,
el hogar de los suicidas,
ellos, los arrepentidos,
están destinados a llorar eternamente,
ellos, los abatidos,
buscarán engañarte para sentirse menos
    solos.
Escúchame, tú, muchacho Mokaya,
Pakujk'tzujk es una flor sin aroma,
la repetición incesante del dolor.
Escúchame, tú, muchacha Mokaya,
Pakujk'tzujk es la tierra
de los que no volverán jamás.

LISTEN, MOKAYA

Sometimes a bit of black ash
floats in from our dreams
and changes the color of the world.
It is a message from Pakujk'tzujk,
home of those who killed themselves,
the unrepentant
destined to cry forever,
the dejected
who try to trick you so they feel less alone.
Listen, young Mokaya man,
Pakujk'tzujk is a scentless flower,
the endless pulsing of pain.
Listen, young Mokaya woman,
Pakujk'tzujk is the land
of those who will never return.

MAKA' TÄ' WYRURAME NHTÄ' 'TUNH'OMO

Nhtä' ujktampa kafel' nhtä' nojatyam'pak' anima',
tese' ponyi'ponyi joko'jinh maka nhkyene
nhtä' sutyaj'papä nhtä' nhtäwäs'nyi'eram.
Maka tä' tujk'wyrurame'
        naptzupä'sawa
            Oko'sawas nhkyut'kuy
Te' no'as syiänh'käis
maka' tä' isanh'tzirame' juwure' te Masanh'kotzäjk:
            Mokayas'tyiäjktam
Te' putzyi'jäyäs yomoma'jinh
maka' nhtä' jampärame' nhtä' ijtkuy Nasakopaj'käsipäna'.
Maka nhtä' tujk'wyrurame'
            Mojk'jäyä
                Nasakopaj'kis'wyenhti.

VOLVEREMOS AL CAMINO

Bebemos café en los velorios
y en cada sorbo se evaporan los rostros
de aquellos a quienes amamos.
Volveremos a ser
     viento de la mañana
          alimento de Oko'sawa.
El resplandor de las velas
nos guiará hacia los sagrados cerros:
    la casa de los Mokayas.
El olor de las flores amarillas
nos hará olvidar lo que hemos sido.
Volveremos a ser
    flor de maíz,
        ofrenda para Nasakopajk'.

RETURNING TO THE PATH

At funeral wakes we drink coffee
and the faces of our beloveds
evaporate with each sip.
We will again become
     the morning breeze
         feeding the Wind Goddess.
The candles' glow will guide us
to sacred mountaintops:
    the Mokayas' home.
The scent of the yellow flowers
will make us forget what we were.
We will again become
    maize flowers,
       an offering for Nasakopajk'.

NOTES ON THE POEMS

"ORE'YOMO"

These poems are about the Chichón (or Pyokpatzyuwe) volcano that rises near Sánchez's hometown—Chapultenango, Chiapas, known locally as Ajway. Gendered female, the volcano is often represented in local art and narrative as aging over the course of each day: a girl in the morning, a young woman in the afternoon, and an old woman at night.

Ore'pät means "Zoque man."

Ore'yomo means "Zoque woman." Both *nkiae* and *syka'e* mean "girl," the latter in the Tapalapa variant of Zoque.

Oko'tzyuwe means "midwife."

Duendes are spirits who live in the forest and care for it.

In many poems, Sánchez refers to naguals, somewhat akin to spirit animals. In Zoque tradition, a person might have several naguals. There isn't a specific relationship between a person's gender and their nagual, though some are considered more masculine and others more feminine. Many factors impact which animal becomes a person's nagual: the date of their birth, their family, and what they are destined to experience in life.

"TO NAME THINGS"

Two

Ipstäjk is one of the three levels of the Zoques' *inframundo*, "inner world," or afterlife. The word translates literally as "twenty houses." Ipstäjk is where the culture-bearers—the dancers, the storytellers, the musicians—go after death. The culture-bearers control the energies that course through the world. Ipstäjk is also a metaphorical place that people can sometimes access through their dreams.

The sower appears frequently in Sánchez's poems, including in this one. There is a community ritual on February 2—the Catholic festival of the Candelaria—that has been adapted as a Zoque celebration of the sowers. The celebration includes a ceremony in which people bring seeds of all the crops that they plant in their fields. There is a dance, and when it ends, the seeds are redistributed to the celebrants.

In Zoque, the same verb is used to refer to planting seeds and to "planting" a human body after death.

Tzitzunh'kotzäjk refers to the Chichón volcano, appending its proper name to the Zoque word for "hill."

The Pinacate are the Pinacate Peaks, located primarily in the Mexican state of Sonora, along the US border in Arizona.

Three

Sánchez frequently references Tzu'anh, another of the three levels of the *inframundo*, this one known as a "permanent fiesta." She explains, "In fact, many who have gone to Tzu'anh remember it like that: mucha fiesta, lots of firecrackers, people eating and dancing."

In the poem, the line "that led me to your unspoken name" refers to the fact that for many years the Zoque people were not permitted by the colonizers to speak the names of their gods aloud.

As is noted in a poem later in this collection, sprigs of black pepper plants are used on altars as an offering to the ancestors and saints.

Four

Women in Ajway don't participate in the traditional Zoque dances. (Though Sánchez has seen a documentary film in which women participated—evidence that they did in the past.) The women's roles in the dances are performed by men dressed as women. Sánchez calls this a "poem of protest" in which the female speaker performs a sacred dance, in honor of the "hidden" Zoque deities mentioned in the last line. Those "hidden gods" were sometimes concealed in plain sight, Sánchez explains. The Dominican priests who long lived in Ajway had Zoque community members carve wooden representations of Catholic saints. It is obvious that these carvings are made in the image of Zoque people (not people of European descent), and they are decorated with iconography taken from ancient Zoque petroglyphs.

Five

The cicada is a sacred creature in Zoque cosmology; to have a cicada as a nagual is an honor. Children are taught not to touch them, in order to protect them. The cicada's song represents the musicians. Everyone who has a cultural role in the Zoque community—musicians, dancers, healers—is visited by a spirit to receive the gift of their community responsibility. In the case of the musicians, a feminine spirit appears in their dreams and gives them flowers. That gift is a sign that they must seek a teacher. The singing of the cicadas is a symbol of this nagual.

Six

There is no direct translation in Zoque for "silence" or "being silent." To represent the concept in Zoque, Sánchez might write "extinguish one's voice" or "absence of words."

Seven

"A dog's tears" is actually morning rheum—the "sleep" that gathers in your eyes. There is a belief in Zoque (and many other) communities that taking the rheum from a dog's eyes and placing it under your own eye gives you the ability to see the dead—those who exist in other dimensions.

Eight

Sánchez takes an ironic tone in this poem, addressing the repression of traditional healing practices.

The Virgin of Carmen appears in this poem, as she appears in the dreams of those who are destined to be healers, bringing them a basket of herbs and flowers that represents the work of healing.

Ten

Many times, when someone becomes ill with *espanto*—which Sánchez says is "one of the most common cultural illnesses"—musicians will play to try and find the source of the espanto so that the person might be cured.

Misyiu'kotzäjk translates as "Cat Mountain."

Teapa, in the Mexican state of Tabasco, is a town north of Sánchez's community and a gateway to her Zoque region.

"MOKAYA"

Kopajktzoka, referenced in several poems in this collection, is a mythological woman, who is often represented as headless.

"THE SOUL RETURNS TO SILENCE'S CRY"

"Ancient coconut water" is meant in the poet's Spanish-language translation to evoke the name of the Grutas de Coconá, a large underground cavern in Tabasco. In Zoque, *koko'nä'* means "deep water," and the cavern, which contains a large cenote, has long been sacred for the Mokaya.

The "night bird" is a metaphor for the hours of sleep that we don't remember. In Zoque communities, elders know that in deepest sleep, they travel to the astral plane.

"RAMA"

Wolof is an Indigenous African language spoken primarily in Senegal, The Gambia, and Mauritania.

"WE'RE ALL MAROONS"

The Mossos d'Esquadra is the police force responsible for law enforcement in the Spanish autonomous community of Catalonia. They are known for hassling immigrant vendors on the streets of Barcelona.

"NEREYDA DREAMED IN NEW YORK"

Tzitzunh refers to the Chichón volcano in this instance, though the word also simply means "mountain" or "hill."

"JESUS NEVER UNDERSTOOD MY GRANDMOTHER'S PRAYERS"

Both *jukis'tyit* and *patzoke* are Zoque-language curse words, meaning "buzzard shit" and "bastard," respectively.

"TO BE ZOQUE IS A PRIVILEGE"

This poem is a sacred song in Zoque, "well established in the Zoque poetic tradition," Sánchez explains. This is the first poem in her 2019 book, a spiritual prelude to the rest of the collection.

Sanhkä, the Zoque word that Sánchez translates as *resplandor* in the Spanish version of the poem, and we render in English as "radiance," is a complex, multidimensional word. In addition to "radiance" it means "enlightened time" and also "understanding"—as distinct from knowledge. *Sanhkä* refers to the cycle of life and references how knowledge is assimilated into a person's life—not the knowledge itself.

"RECEPTION FOR A MOKAYA MAN"

This poem is in the voice of a hailer, a person hired to invoke certain words and phrases, to bring about a certain event. It's not as common a tradition as it once was in Sánchez's community, but it still exists. For example, Sánchez was the seventh girl to be born to her family. After her birth, her father asked a hailer to come to her house and invoke the words to bring the family a son. The next child born to her parents was a boy.

"RECEPTION FOR A MOKAYA WOMAN"

The three Thunderbolt Men referenced in this poem are naguals, representing red, yellow, and white lightning. These naguals have great power—they control the climate, and they have the power to see the future. The Thunderbolt Men live in Ipstäjk, the level of the inner world where the culture bearers go after death.

"MY FATHER GAVE ME A GIFT"

The *wewe* is a large yellow flower, similar to a bird of paradise, endemic to the high rainforest near Sánchez's community. When you move the parts of the flower, it makes a series of squeaks that sound like birdsong. People bring *wewes* back from the forest for their babies and small children to play with, so they can learn how to make the sounds that will enable them to speak.

"WEWE"

Nhkirawa is the Zoque word for a foreigner, outsider, or (generally) a white person. The term is occasionally also used to refer to community members who "think like foreigners," Sánchez says.

"FEAST"

There are many stories in Zoque communities about gophers. For example, children who are abandoned by their parents are said to transform themselves into gophers and live underground. They steal the crops because, as children, they don't yet know how to work for their own food. The campesinos don't kill the gophers when they find them in their fields, because they understand the creatures must feed themselves.

"CEIBA"

This poem refers to the silk-cotton tree (ceiba), which is sacred to the Zoque people. The ceiba is also the tree from which the Spanish conquistadors hanged Zoque ancestors who refused to convert to Christianity.

"LISTEN, MOKAYA"

This poem begins with a reference to the ash left after the Chichón volcano exploded in 1982—the worst natural disaster of the century in Mexico and an event that deeply marked life for Sánchez's home region.

Acknowledgments

English translations in this book were previously published in the following periodicals and anthologies, often in a slightly different form. The poet and co-translators are grateful to all these journals and their editors.

The third poem of the series "To Name Things," as well as "Returning to the Path," appear in the anthology *Daughters of Latin America: An International Anthology of Writing by Latine Women* (HarperCollins, 2023).

The twelve poems in the series "Mokaya" appear in the anthology *Temporary Archives: Poems by Women of Latin America* (Arc Edge Hill, 2022). The first four poems of this series also appeared in *Modern Poetry in Translation* (2021).

Several of the poems in the series "The Soul Returns to Silence's Cry" appeared in the anthology *Like a New Sun: New Indigenous Mexican Poetry* (Phoneme, 2015) and in the journal *Bengal Lights* (2013).

"[Yesterday]" and "[I want to join the pilgrimage of butterflies]" appeared in *World Literature Today* (2023).

"Aisha" appeared in the premiere issue of *The Los Angeles Press* (2017) and in *Bengal Lights* (2013).

"Rama" appeared in *Bitter Oleander* (2014).

"Nereyda Dreamed in New York" appeared in *World Literature Today* (2014) and *Latin American Literature Today* (2017).

"[Death will arrive / and find you in your bed]," "[Death will arrive / the true one]," "[May just one prayer]," and "[Those who sleep beyond day and night]" appeared in *Drunken Boat* (2014).

"[One day a man]" appeared in *Like a New Sun: New Indigenous Mexican Poetry* (Phoneme, 2015).

"Jesus Never Understood My Grandmother's Prayers," appeared in *World Literature Today* (2014) and *Latin American Literature Today* (2017), as well as in the anthologies *Like a New Sun* and *Poems from the Edge of Extinction: An Anthology of Poetry in Endangered Languages* (Chambers, 2019).

"My Father Gave Me a Gift" appeared in *Poetry* Magazine (2022).

"How to Be a Good Savage" appeared in *Pleiades* (2020) and in the anthology *Temporary Archives*.

"Saspalanki's Children Cry in the Big City" appeared in *Pleiades* (2020).

"We Are Millions" appeared in *World Literature Today* (2019).

"What Is It Worth?" appeared in *Modern Poetry in Translation* (2019) and in the anthologies *Staying Human* (Bloodaxe, 2020) and *Temporary Archives*.

Both translators and author are grateful to the entire team at Milkweed for their care and enthusiasm for this book. Wendy Call would also like to thank Adela Ramos for her invaluable feedback on many of the English translations.

Israel Gutiérrez

MIKEAS SÁNCHEZ is one of the most important poets of the Indigenous Americas, working in Zoque, a language spoken in southern Mexico. She is the only woman to have ever published a book of poetry in that language. Her six volumes of poetry—including *Mojk'jäyä / Mokaya* and *Mumure' nhtä' yäjktampä / Todos somos cimarrones*—are all bilingual Zoque-Spanish. Sánchez's work has been translated into Bangla, Catalan, English, German, Italian, Maya, Mixe, and Portuguese. In Chiapas, Mexico, she was awarded first place in the "Y el Bolóm dice . . ." Prize for Fiction as well as the Pat O'tan Prize for Indigenous Poetry. Sánchez is a radio producer, translator, community health promoter, and defender of Zoque lands. She lives in Ajway, Chiapas.

Axel Rivera

WENDY CALL is co-editor of *Telling True Stories: A Nonfiction Writers'*
Guide and *Best Literary Translations*, author of the award-winning *No*
Word for Welcome, and translator of two collections of poetry by Mexican-
Zapotec poet Irma Pineda: *In the Belly of Night and Other Poems* and
Nostalgia Doesn't Flow Away Like Riverwater. Her literary projects have
been supported by Artist Trust, the Fulbright Commission, and the
National Endowment for the Arts. Call serves on the faculty of the
Rainier Writing Workshop MFA program and lives in Seattle, on
Duwamish land, and in Oaxaca, Mexico, on Mixtec and Zapotec land.

Travis Elborough

SHOOK is a poet, translator, and editor whose work has spanned a wide range of languages and places. Their writing has appeared in *Poetry*, *World Literature Today*, the *Guardian*, and many other publications, as well as being translated into more than a dozen languages, including Isthmus Zapotec, Kurdish, and Uyghur. Since founding Phoneme Media in 2013, Shook has edited and published translations from over thirty-five languages. Today they direct Kashkul Books, a publishing project based in the Kurdistan Region of Iraq, as well as the translation-focused imprint avión at Gato Negro Ediciones in Mexico City. They reside at Newt Beach, on Coast Miwok land in West Marin.

ABOUT SEEDBANK

Just as repositories around the world gather seeds in an effort to ensure biodiversity in the future, Seedbank gathers works of literature from around the world that foster reflection on the relationship of human beings with place and the natural world.

SEEDBANK FOUNDERS

The generous support of the following visionary investors makes this series possible:

Meg Anderson and David Washburn

Anonymous

The Hlavka Family

milkweed
EDITIONS

Founded as a nonprofit organization in 1980, Milkweed Editions is an independent publisher. Our mission is to identify, nurture, and publish transformative literature, and build an engaged community around it.

Milkweed Editions is based in Bdé Óta Othúŋwe (Minneapolis) within Mní Sota Makhóčhe, the traditional homeland of the Dakhóta people. Residing here since time immemorial, Dakhóta people still call Mní Sota Makhóčhe home, with four federally recognized Dakhóta nations and many more Dakhóta people residing in what is now the state of Minnesota. Due to continued legacies of colonization, genocide, and forced removal, generations of Dakhóta people remain disenfranchised from their traditional homeland. Presently, Mní Sota Makhóčhe has become a refuge and home for many Indigenous nations and peoples, including seven federally recognized Ojibwe nations. We humbly encourage our readers to reflect upon the historical legacies held in the lands they occupy.

milkweed.org

Milkweed Editions, an independent nonprofit publisher, gratefully acknowledges sustaining support from our Board of Directors; the Alan B. Slifka Foundation and its president, Riva Ariella Ritvo-Slifka; the Amazon Literary Partnership; the Ballard Spahr Foundation; Copper Nickel; the McKnight Foundation; the National Endowment for the Arts; the National Poetry Series; and other generous contributions from foundations, corporations, and individuals. Also, this activity is made possible by the voters of Minnesota through a Minnesota State Arts Board Operating Support grant, thanks to a legislative appropriation from the arts and cultural heritage fund. For a full listing of Milkweed Editions supporters, please visit milkweed.org.

Interior design by Mary Austin Speaker
Typeset in Adobe Caslon Pro

Adobe Caslon Pro was created by Carol Twombly
for Adobe Systems in 1990. Her design was inspired by
the family of typefaces cut by the celebrated engraver
William Caslon I, whose family foundry served
England with clean, elegant type from the early
Enlightenment through the turn of the
twentieth century.